CHANGE YOUR LIFE 3-IN-1 COLLECTION

BUCKET LIST BLUEPRINT, SUPER SEXY GOAL
SETTING, FIND YOUR PURPOSE IN 15 MINUTES

JULIE SCHOOLER

DISCLAIMER

This book is designed to give the reader (that means YOU – the exceptionally awesome person reading this!) some useful tips and ideas about how to create and act upon your bucket list, set goals and find your purpose.

It does not replace expert advice from medical or behavioral specialists. It is recommended that you seek advice from qualified professionals if you are concerned in any way.

Taking action to improve your life may pose some risk. The author and publisher advise readers to take full responsibility for their safety and know their limits.

What this means for YOU:

- Talk to a health professional before embarking on any increased physical activity.
- Make sure you have full and correct insurance (travel, health, etc.) whenever required.
- Use common sense to keep safe when traveling locally or abroad, and research safety measures that are appropriate in other countries or regions.
- Make sure any equipment you use has been well-maintained.
- Choose reputable companies with the best safety records.
- Tell someone where you are going, what you are doing, and when you expect to be back.
- Choose bucket list and goals items that are within your means financially or for which you are prepared to budget and save.

- Make responsible arrangements so that your work, family and other important areas of life remain in good condition while you pursue your bucket list, take action on your goals and find your purpose.

Please, please, please do not choose irresponsible, destructive or illegal items.

The author and publisher accept no responsibility for any harm or loss resulting from taking action to improve your life.

Have fun but keep safe.

This Change Your Life 3-in-1 Collection is dedicated to Andrew, Natalie and Eloise

CONTENTS

Reader Gift: The Happy20   ix

BUCKET LIST BLUEPRINT   1
SUPER SEXY GOAL SETTING   99
FIND YOUR PURPOSE IN 15 MINUTES   199

Reader Gift: The Happy20   315
About the Author   317
Books by Julie Schooler   319
Acknowledgments   321
Please Leave a Review   323
Book References   325

READER GIFT: THE HAPPY20

There is no doubt that creating a bucket list, setting goals and finding your purpose will change your life, but it is also important to remember to squeeze the best out every single day. To remind you of this, I created

THE HAPPY20
20 Free Ways to Boost Happiness in 20 Seconds or Less

A PDF gift for you with quick ideas to improve mood and add a little sparkle to your day.

Head to **JulieSchooler.com/gift** and grab your copy today.

- A NOURISH YOUR SOUL BOOK -

BLUEPRINT

EVERYTHING YOU NEED TO START A BUCKET LIST THAT BRINGS YOUR DREAMS TO LIFE

JULIE SCHOOLER

BUCKET LIST BLUEPRINT

Everything You Need to Start a Bucket List That Brings Your Dreams to Life

-A *Nourish Your Soul* Book-

Julie Schooler

CONTENTS

1. Boring To Breathtaking   7
2. What Is A Bucket List And Is It For Me?   13
3. Bucket List Objections   19
4. Why You Absolutely Need A Bucket List   27
5. Seven Unexpected Benefits Of A Bucket List   33
6. Write Your Bucket List   41
7. Bucket List Q&A   49
8. Organize Your Bucket List   57
9. Check Off The First Bucket List Item   65
10. Bucket Lists With Family And Friends   73
11. Supercharge Your Bucket List   79
12. Bucket List Wrap Up   87

Appendix One - My Top40 Bucket List   91
Appendix Two – A Selection of Bucket List Ideas   93
Appendix Three – Bucket List 100 Items Template   97

1

BORING TO BREATHTAKING

 'The tragedy of life is not death but what we let die inside of us while we live.' – Norman Cousins

What Happened to 'Carpe Diem'?

Each day blends into the next. The same old routine. You have nothing exciting to look forward to. Life seems bland. What is worse is that the days seem to be going by in a blur. Life is rushing by at what seems like an increasing speed each year.

You know there is a bigger life to live. You would love to do something exciting or challenging or meaningful with the good years you have left on this planet. You yearn to get off the rapid and repetitive treadmill of life and actually LIVE. You want to 'carpe diem', seize the day!

But how do you start taking action towards the life of your dreams? What is the first step to planning a life well lived? You need a guide to help you determine what you DO want in life, not what you don't want.

You NEED a bucket list.

Spring Out of Bed Each Morning

This book will give you practical advice to write the best bucket list personalized for your circumstances, and, most importantly, how to check off items immediately so that you start living the life you always dreamed of.

This entertaining and easy-to-read guide will also cut through the confusion around what a bucket list is and is not, provide compelling reasons why a bucket list is an essential part of life and tell you exactly what to do to discover items for your personal bucket list—even if you have no money, no time and don't want to travel.

In less than a couple of hours this book will give you the exact blueprint to writing your own bucket list. You won't need to spend hours searching for information all over the Internet. You will have a clear direction and won't be confused by conflicting advice. Your new, personalized bucket list will help you spring out of bed every morning with renewed enthusiasm for living, not just existing.

Your life will become breathtaking, not boring.

The Top40 Bucket List Challenge

I turned 40 in 2016. This milestone birthday was a catalyst for a big, hairy, audacious goal: check off 40 things from my bucket list in one calendar year. Hence I took on a major challenge—what I called the 'Top40 Bucket List'.

My life is great and I feel extremely blessed with what I have: a lovely suburban home, a kind husband and two loud but gorgeous kids. But a deep desire to do something extra special to mark turning the big 4-0 could not be contained. I wanted to see what it was like to reach my potential, to step out of my comfort zone and to live life even more fully.

I had to work out what bucket list items I wanted to do, then narrow it down to ones that would be possible to do within my time, resources and budget. I read up on how to write bucket lists, got ideas from searching all over the Internet and asked for a lot of help from friends and family.

Surprisingly, I could not find one short, clear, gimmick-free guide on how to write and check off a bucket list, whether over the course of one year or for the rest of my life. I had to scramble around, wasting time trying to work out all these things. A practical blueprint on bucket lists would have made my challenge much easier to manage. I could have started actually doing the things on my bucket list earlier. I also made a lot of mistakes in executing the bucket list and would have done it differently if I had a clear guide.

I distilled the avalanche of information and all my learnings from my Top40 Bucket List challenge into simple and practical tips to help you write your bucket list and then take action to check it off. You gain the best insights and avoid common mistakes around bucket lists. This book contains all the tools, advice and inspiration you need to live a fulfilling and immensely enjoyable life.

Whether you want to do one, ten or a hundred things on a bucket list, and whether you plan to do them in the next week, next year or over the rest of the time you have, this book will help you work out, write out, and most importantly, achieve your heart's desires.

I have written the book that I wanted to read.

Benefits of a Bucket List

Just think how great it will be when you have a written bucket list and you are crossing off items. There are benefits in so many areas. You will:

- rediscover long-held passions and understand your true self better
- know exactly how to determine what you want in life, not what you don't want
- feel good about yourself for following through on goals
- learn and grow by stepping out of your comfort zone
- wake up each morning with a sense of excitement and zest for life
- spend quality time with friends and family doing fun things together
- lead and inspire others to live life on their terms
- feel like you are living the life you were meant to live, one with excitement, meaning and true joy

The Only Bucket List Book You Will Ever Need

People are happy to recommend this book as it contains everything you need and nothing you don't around bucket lists. They are excited that there is a finally a short book that helps them to easily write and take action on their perfect bucket lists.

Readers are relieved that this book has removed the old association of bucket lists only being for the terminally ill and has made them for anyone. From adrenaline junkies to those more interested in leisurely pursuits, there are tips and ideas that will suit any age, budget and preference.

My Promise to You

This book will make it stress-free and fun to write the bucket list of your dreams. In addition, I promise that you will easily find 100 things for your bucket list that suit your circumstances so perfectly that you will check off at least one item before you even finish reading the book!

It is guaranteed that if you use this book to write a bucket list, you will feel better, family times will be fun again and you will give yourself the best gift of all—a fulfilling life.

Your Ideal Life is Waiting

Do not leave it another dreary and mundane day to read this book. Be the happy, energized and accomplished person you always thought you would be—not when you are too old or ill to do anything, but right now. Read this book today and take action on your ideal life.

Read this Before You Kick the Bucket

Step off the dull treadmill of day-to-day life and turn your dreams into memories. Don't wait until you almost 'kick the bucket' to read this book! Bucket lists are for the living, not the nearly dead. Start now, before you are too sick and frail to enjoy anything.

This book will reignite that spark you once had. You will learn how to focus on what you really want—to live a life by design, not by default. Ultimately, this bucket list book will lead you to be more enriched, fulfilled and happy, every single day, for the rest of your life.

2

WHAT IS A BUCKET LIST AND IS IT FOR ME?

 'We live, we die, and the wheels on the bus go round and round.' – Edward Cole, played by Jack Nicholson, in the film *The Bucket List*

WHAT IS A BUCKET LIST?

A bucket list is a record of the most important things you want to do, dreams you want to fulfill, special items you want to have or own, people you want to meet, and experiences, accomplishments and challenges you want to overcome in your lifetime.

In short, a bucket list is a list of things you want to do before you die. Actually, let's add one word into the shorter definition.

A bucket list is a WRITTEN list of things you want to do before you die

The writing down part is an essential element of a bucket list. More on writing and its importance later.

The 'bucket' part comes from the expression 'kick the bucket', which is a euphemism for dying, although no one quite knows why that association was made. A bucket list, therefore, is closely linked with a terminal diagnosis or being old and sick. The term was popularized in the 2007 film *The Bucket List* starring Jack Nicholson and Morgan Freeman.

Removing this association with imminent mortality is one of the main objectives of this book. Sure, we are all going to die, but a bucket list can—and should—be written by anyone, especially those of us who are fortunate enough to be alive and well.

A hot air balloon ride is a 'classic' bucket list item. One hot air balloon operator admitted that he gives half-price rides to terminal cancer patients as he gets so many enquiries from them. That is one of the saddest things I have ever heard. Please, please book your hot air balloon trip when you are not sick, even if it does cost you full price. Believe me, it is worth every penny.

We are all going to die one day, so you can't ignore your own mortality, but creating a bucket list need not be linked so tightly to it. Hopefully picking up this book will inspire you to start yours today, not when you are nearly dead.

> Having a bucket list isn't about dying.
> It is about living.

WHO IS THIS BOOK FOR AND NOT FOR?

I don't want to waste your time, so I will be as straight up as possible about whom this book is for and not for and how you should read it.

This book is for anyone from 9 to 90 who wants to live a more fulfilling and fun life. As noted above, it is not just for the terminally ill or nearly dead. That is an out-of-date association. The new bucket list definition is a rejuvenated and inclusive one for everyone.

Bucket lists are NOT for you if you just want to follow the same old routine day in and day out. They are NOT for you if you only want to do what society expects of you. And they are certainly NOT for you if you simply want to work hard and delay your enjoyment of life until you are old and retired.

This book and bucket lists in general ARE for you if you want a challenge, desire some adventure and need some variety in your life. Chapter Four discusses the deep human need for variety in depth. A bucket list is for anyone who is still curious about life and who has a mindset of wanting to experiment. This sense of just trying things out means that sometimes you will fail at things and sometimes things don't happen as you would like, and you will learn to deal with that.

Most importantly, this book will help you create a bucket list so you don't get to the end of your life with regrets. The main regrets of the dying will be touched on later, but for now, let's keep it light and say that bucket lists are for people who want to create great memories.

Be the person at the office with the interesting weekend story of riding on a tandem bike or learning to surf. Enjoy planning that trip to the Tuscan cooking school you have always dreamed about. And look forward to recounting that time you became a clown for a day or were an extra in a movie to your grandchildren.

· · ·

The Top40 Bucket List

One morning, not long after I turned 39, I woke up with a ridiculous idea. I am turning 40. There are at least 40 things on my bucket list. I could attempt to check off 40 bucket list items in a year. Some of those may not be possible, but I could get more ideas. I quickly started scouring the Internet for inspiration and asking friends for suggestions.

I knew deep in my bones that this was what I wanted to do in order to embrace this birthday milestone. I was excited. My 'Top40 Bucket List' was born. Some items were cheap, local, and even dull. 'Grow sunflowers' was one item that would seem modest to others. Some I had to plan and budget for—traveling to another city to see 'The World of Wearable Arts' was one of the more expensive and time consuming items. I definitely had to consider finances, family commitments and other constraints, but I had a list of 40 bucket list items I was intent on checking off.

What a way to celebrate turning 40!

You probably have two immediate questions—what were these 40 items and did I succeed in doing them all? The Top40 Bucket List is listed in Appendix One, but don't peek just yet. I said don't peek! You will be writing your own bucket list soon, and it is better not to have too many ideas from someone else inside your brain when you do. Look at my list after you take a stab at the first draft of your bucket list.

For now, know that—spoiler alert—YES! I succeeded in checking off every single one of the 40 bucket list items during 2016. I ended on a literal high note when on the 30th of December 2016, I jumped out of a plane in a tandem skydive.

·   ·   ·

Why I Wrote This Book

It was a LOT of hard work figuring out the exact 40 items to do, writing them down, scheduling them in and working out how to take action on them. I had to adjust around travel, budget and family constraints, keep motivated all year long and overcome a lot of fear (tandem skydives are not for the faint hearted!).

What made it harder was that I had absolutely no frame of reference. You will still have to figure out your own bucket list and face your fears; no one can do that for you. But now that you have this book in your hands, coming up with your own personal bucket list—and of course, starting it and checking it off—will be much easier for you.

I wrote this book so that the next person who wants to prioritize a bit of fun or embrace some new challenges can write their perfect bucket list. They don't have to do something crazy like cross off 40 items in a year, but knowing they are moving towards even one long held wish is exciting.

This book is here to help you focus on what you really want. You will feel a major sense of achievement in marking off items. And you will grow as a person as you step out of your comfort zone and complete a challenge that was only a dream.

If you are a 'get to the point' person, then feel free to skip the next three chapters and go straight to Chapter Six. That plus Chapters Seven, Eight and Nine are the main ones you will need to create your own best bucket list and start taking action on it. However, if you still need a bit more convincing about why a bucket list is not only a good idea, but essential to a life well lived, keep reading right through.

This is a short book but—and this is not said lightly—it <u>will</u> change your life.

3

BUCKET LIST OBJECTIONS

 'Life isn't about finding yourself. Life is about creating yourself.' – George Bernard Shaw

But But But

You are aged between 9 and 90, you want some more fun and adventure, and you kind of like the idea of a little book that will change your life. BUUUUUUTTTTT, you still have some objections to this whole bucket list malarkey. Boy, you are a hard nut to crack! Let's address these objections up front now so we can keep moving to the good bits, shall we?

'It feels like another To-Do list and I have one of those already (that I don't do)'

Contrary to the fact that it has 'list' in its name, a bucket list is NOT a to-do list. Think of it more as a 'capture list' or a 'priority list'. It is where you write down your most important dreams and goals to make you feel happier and more fulfilled. You are pinpointing what you really want in life and in a way excluding (for now at least) what you don't want.

We live in a time in which we have the technology, transport and resources to help us go anywhere and do anything, but no one can 'do it all'. Your bucket list will tap into your deepest desires and help you focus on the best things in life for you. It will only become a TO-DO when you schedule it in your diary or calendar.

'IT SOUNDS GREAT, BUT DON'T HAVE TIME RIGHT NOW FOR A BUCKET list'

Oh yes, the time excuse. The old cliché of 'work' and 'family' taking priority. Let's counter these jaded responses with some equally tired but oh so incredibly true sayings. You only live once. Life is not a dress rehearsal. Let me remind you that if you are happier, then others around you will be, too, and you will be better at what you do.

Look, we all have the same 24 hours in a day, and someone out there is swimming with whales and you are not. You are busy being busy without adding value into your life.

> Our culture celebrates busyness!
> Don't confuse this with living a fulfilling life.

How many times have you checked Facebook or Twitter already today? What if in those few seconds, you looked up flights to Paris, or how many days at Disney World are recommended, or how much a Caribbean cruise would cost?

You can spend a lot of time focusing on other people in social media, but wouldn't it feel a lot better if you directed your attention onto little tasks to put in place a dream trip? You may not have time for travel now, but you do have spare moments in the day in which you can plan your next vacation.

To actually complete bucket list items, you could do things on your bucket list as a family. Take the kids rock climbing or learn origami together. Or you can stack bucket list items together. This will be discussed in a later chapter, but for example, when I wrote down that I wanted to see the 'The World of Wearable Arts' in Wellington, I found a couple of other things to do in Wellington and added them to my bucket list.

Overall, delegate or eliminate things in your life that are not top priority. Say "no" in the nicest possible way. Push your bucket list to the front, or you will end up doing it when you are nearly dead, or not at all.

'I can't think of things for my bucket list'

Don't worry, you have come to the right place. There are plenty of questions and exercises in here to prompt your imagination. In addition, there are ways to think about your bucket list in terms of categories that will help get the brainstorming going.

There is also a little-known thing called the 'Internet' and that does have a lot of ideas as well. Your imagination may need a little nudge as it has been swamped by boring daily routines and you have forgotten how to be child-like and playful. At the moment, don't worry about having no ideas. By the end of this book you will have plenty.

'I want to do everything'

You may think you want to do everything. The Internet may be to blame here as you can see everything is possible. Visit every country in the world. Taste all the different foods. As Julie Andrews sings: 'Climb Every Mountain'. Again, I would contend this is due to your creativity being stifled. You want everything because that is easier than thinking in specifics about what you really want.

If it helps, start writing a 'NOT bucket list'. People often find it easier to know what they don't want to do. I knew there was no way I would be ever be coaxed into doing a bungy jump. No way. Never. What are your never evers? Strangely, this will help filter down to more specific bucket list ideas that you actually do want to do.

'I don't have the money for a bucket list'

First, remember this is a capture list; you are not scheduling anything just yet. And second, there are hundreds of ideas you can do for very little or no money. Over half of the ideas on my Top40 Bucket List cost under $200. Many were free. Only one cost over $1,000.

With regard to travel, you can use air points or reward points and look for good deals. Remember also that budgeting becomes easier and more fun with a specific travel goal in mind. Or you can use your bucket list items to save you money—a two-for-one deal. Creating a special signature dish with your own secret recipe will save you the cost of takeaways or eating out. Teaching yourself the ukulele or mastering a card trick are simple and low-cost ideas to do at home. Deciding to run a marathon will keep you fit without the expensive gym fees. Think outside the box.

. . .

'Isn't a bucket list a 'nice to have' rather than an essential part of life?'

Another way of saying this objection is, "What is the point of a bucket list? It seems kind of frivolous."

A bucket list is as far from silly or shallow as you can get. In fact, it is not really about doing all those external things at all. A bucket list taps into your deepest wants and desires. It allows you to get out of your comfort zone and therefore grow as a person. And it gives you a sense of discipline in planning, plus a feeling of accomplishment in achieving items on the list.

> You don't just take away memories, but a surer sense of self, and that is priceless.

'Shouldn't I focus on the journey, not the destination?'

In our busy-centric world we focus on neither the journey nor the destination! At least having a bucket list puts an end goal in sight. It is well documented that successful people begin with the end in mind, so maybe the classic 'journey' argument is not that important.

Luckily with bucket lists, as well as a goal, there is a lot of journey involved. You can use spare moments to plan larger bucket list items and your anticipation of an upcoming event is an invaluable source of happiness. (More about this later.) Don't use whether the journey or destination is better as an excuse not to have a bucket list at all.

'I don't want everything I do planned out. Where is the spontaneity?'

Some objectors will say that making a clear list allows no room for spontaneity in life. Having a list of set goals takes all the fun out of it. But without any goals there is no fun to start with!

You can still be spontaneous, but at least with a bucket list already prepared, you will have an inkling of the type of activities and experiences you want to do. If something comes up that is not on the list but speaks to you, then write it down and do it as well. If you are at the beach for surf lessons and notice that there are jet skis for hire, then go for it! You can change your bucket list at any time.

'ISN'T HAVING A BUCKET LIST KIND OF SELFISH?'

Having a bucket list is a way of taking action to increase your happiness, connect with others and grow as a person through undertaking challenges. It is one of the least selfish things you can ever do!

Creating a bucket list enables you to rediscover long held dreams and find out more about your authentic self. It also shows you as an action taker, a person who puts themselves out there and is prepared to fail. In other words, it shows that you are a leader, and goodness knows, we need more positive role models in leadership.

Yes, at times when I was arranging yet another weekend around a Top40 Bucket List item, I felt a bit self-centered. But without the list driving me, my family and I wouldn't have had a picnic on that little-known island close by, my husband and I would have had a sedate date night instead of riding on a tandem bike together, and I certainly wouldn't have spent money at businesses in other cities. Doing the Top40 Bucket List made me a better person, and I also got to spend quality time with friends and family. Where is the selfish part in that?

If that still doesn't convince you, then link some of your bucket list items to charitable endeavors such as doing a fun run that sponsors a charity. Or put down 'work in a soup kitchen for a day', 'give blood' or 'learn CPR' as things you would like to do.

'Isn't a bucket list risky?'

A bucket list does have a risk element to it. There is no denying that. But it has about the same amount of risk as life itself. None of us gets out of here alive! You need to balance wanting to live life as fully as possible with your tolerance for risk.

There is a disclaimer at the start of this book and it will be recapped here. Talk to a health professional before embarking on any change in physical activity. Make sure you have full and correct insurance. Use common sense to keep safe while traveling. Choose reputable companies with the best safety records. Please do not put highly dangerous, irresponsible or illegal items on your list. The ideas in this book are only suggestions. Ultimately, the choices you make for your bucket list are entirely your responsibility.

What You Are Really Saying

Most of the questions and statements above, especially the last one, are your mind's attempts to procrastinate and tell you a bucket list is 'too hard' because there is fear involved.

These objections are a way of saying you are scared. And that is natural. Of course you are scared. Scared of failing. Scared of stepping out of your comfort zone. Scared of doing things that are not 'normal' in our society. A bit of fear is healthy and won't miraculously disappear. More on fear in the next chapter, but for now understand that the only way to eliminate fear is to <u>do</u> the thing you fear.

We have covered many, if not all, of your objections, but we are not done with the dark parts yet. The next chapter explains why most people will never write a bucket list even though they absolutely need one.

4

WHY YOU ABSOLUTELY NEED A BUCKET LIST

 'In the end what matters is how much happiness they have brought to those they love and how much time they spent doing things they themselves loved.' – Bronnie Ware

NEGATIVE THINKING

What has stopped you from living the life of your dreams?

The reason you are not doing what you want in life is because of your thoughts. Your thoughts are just thoughts. They are not real things but only whispers and conversations inside your mind. Most people's thoughts are about 80% negative.

> Most people think about what they don't want.

So if your mind is shaping your future, but all you are thinking about is what you don't want, then the world around you gives you exactly that. So you get less fun and challenge in your life because you don't want to feel scared. You get less time for your hobbies and passions because you don't want to look out of place or not serious enough. You get less opportunity to explore, as you don't want to leave your comfort zone.

You don't live the life of your dreams because your silly, little, negative, untruthful thoughts tell you that they are impossible and no one lives like that.

Let's get this straight right now: you are responsible for your life; you create your life. Not the latest political scandal, not climate change, not a nuclear or terrorism threat. You. If you are just going through the motions in life controlled by fear, then it is up to you to find a way to change that. Hint: picking up this book is a very good start.

You may be kicking yourself right about now, but know that everyone is like this until they wake up.

It ends today! Don't let the story you tell yourself stop you from being truly happy and fulfilled.

The Comfort Zone

For example, people think they don't want to leave their comfort zones, as they feel nice and familiar, and they feel safe and in control of their environments. Going to work, coming back to your home, watching TV, these are all nice at times. Being in your comfort zone is comfortable, but after a while it actually starts to hurt you. You start to feel unenthused and jaded with your routine existence.

Stepping out of your comfort zone and trying new things leads to growth, and growth is necessary for a fulfilling life. More about this below but hopefully this gives you a little taste of what changing one negative thought can do to improve your life.

The real magic happens outside of the comfort zone. So if the magic happens there, why do you want to stay inside your comfort zone? It is because of your NEED for certainty.

The Six Human Needs

Author, coach and personal development expert, Tony Robbins, has popularized the theory that we all have six human needs. These are needs, not wants. We crave these on a deep level.

We have a need for **certainty**—to feel safe and secure and to know that our expectations will be met. In apparent opposition to this, we have a need for **variety**—to have surprises and excitement in our lives (taking a vacation, for example). We also have a need for **significance**—to feel important and that our lives have meaning. On the other side of the coin, we have a need for **love and connection**. We can't be too individual, too significant, or we often lose connection with others.

These four needs are our core or personality needs. The other two needs are for **growth** and **contribution**. These are our secondary or spiritual needs, and not everyone gets these two needs met as the other four can take priority. This is an extremely concise description, and I encourage every one of you to look up Tony Robbins's explanation of these needs in more detail.

Many people intuitively sense a truth in 'The Six Human Needs'. But you don't even have to believe it. They run your life regardless of whether you think they do or not. How you try and meet these needs—in positive, negative or neutral ways—plus which needs you emphasize, have a major impact on your life.

The Needs for Certainty and Variety

The need that pervades life the most is the need for certainty. People innately want to feel safe, secure, and yes, comfortable. You desire control, order and predictability because you think your life depends on it. And, as demonstrated with the insight into comfort zones above, this is helpful, to a degree, but it can also be harmful.

Your need for certainty helps you find stable work, a place to live, and it builds your family and community around you, but it also allows you to fall into the same routine and you get bored. You get bored because you have another equally important need; the need for variety, but it often gets ignored or minimized, as certainty is so tremendously important to you.

The need for variety is why you have vacation time. It is the reason workweeks have weekends attached. It is why people make time for hobbies. You need to prioritize it just as much as certainty or you stay the same and don't grow, and then life becomes a monotonous, dull effort. Think how great you feel after you spend a weekend away. Only a couple of days and you have a renewed energy and zest for life.

> One of the best things about a bucket list is that it meets your deep needs for certainty and variety at the same time.

Certainty: You get to organize your thoughts, plan things you want to cross off and have a system for doing things you always wanted to do.

Variety: you get to do new things, expand your world and challenge yourself. You thought a bucket list was an extra, a 'nice to have' thing in your life and now you realize it is absolutely essential for meeting two of your primary needs.

So why do people let the need for certainty override their equally important need for variety? Why do people not like change? Because of their deeply ingrained fears.

Fear and Death

Some people are better at dealing with fears than others, but we ALL have fear. We fear different things, but ultimately, as Susan Jeffers points out in her classic self-help book *Feel the Fear and Do It Anyway*, we have an underlying fear of 'I can't handle it'. We fear that we can't handle whatever life brings us.

This makes sense in relation to our fear of death. We fear death because although it is inevitable, we are not sure when it will happen, whether it will be painful and how our loved ones will cope without us. It is very important, therefore, to stop and discuss death for a little bit, as checking off a bucket list is—for better or worse—intrinsically linked to death, or its euphemism, 'kicking the bucket'.

Because we fear death, we shut out the very prospect of it. We need to stop pretending that we will live forever, that we have all the time in the world, and face our own mortality straight on. Although I don't like bucket lists to be associated with terminal diagnoses, perhaps remembering that in one way or another, we are all 'terminal' will help us live life more fully.

> Time is limited, whether we deny that fact or not.

In the end, we all need to face up to our very real mortality. Let us dance with our fear of death. That will move our energies from a material life of comfort controlled by fear to a life of purpose, fulfillment and fun. Start with accepting the limited days you have left and then think about what you really want out of life.

The alternative to designing a fulfilling life is coming to the end of your life with regrets. People can regret a whole range of things, but, as noted in Bronnie Ware's book, *The Top Five Regrets of the Dying*, many people wish they had lived a life that was more true to who they were, let themselves be happier and not worked so hard. Starting your own bucket list will go a long way towards eliminating these regrets from your own deathbed.

Do you want to keep on having the same life you have had so far, securely ensconced in your tiny comfort zone, prioritizing your need for certainty and controlled by your fears so much that you die with regrets? Or do you want to live life on your terms, working out and then taking action on what your heart desires?

This will be said a few times in this book, but you have choices. You can choose to live in fear and not do the things you want to do most in life then die with regrets, OR you can choose to face your fears, dance with them and ultimately eliminate them by doing what you love. Both choices are hard. Choose your hard.

If all this talk of stepping out of your comfort zone, embracing your need for variety and facing your fear of dying doesn't persuade you to create your bucket list straight away, then the next chapter will seal the deal with seven unexpected benefits of having a bucket list.

SEVEN UNEXPECTED BENEFITS OF A BUCKET LIST

 'It is not the years in your life but the life in your years that counts.' - Adlai E. Stevenson

THE SUPER SEVEN

Here are seven, perhaps slightly unexpected, benefits of a bucket list:

1. A BUCKET LIST BUILDS INTEGRITY

In order to create a bucket list, you must work first at brainstorming about what you want. As noted earlier, this is hard as most people are thinking about what they don't want. Then you need to prioritize what you are able to do and when you will do it. As you have access to everything in life, the ability to focus and prioritize is now a rare and highly sought after skill. Then you actually have to execute your plan, which is perhaps the most difficult step of all.

All these stages to a bucket list create diligence and conscientiousness and ultimately show integrity—in that you do what you say you are going to do. It shows you plan, take action and follow through to the end. Integrity is an extraordinary trait these days. Other people—friends, work colleagues and especially your kids—appreciate and are inspired by it, and you get to feel great about yourself as well.

Doing my Top40 Bucket List was a mighty challenge, stressful and hard work at times, but even now I still feel proud and extremely satisfied that I crossed it all off.

2. A Bucket List Allows You to Fail

You may be worried about creating a bucket list and then never marking it all off. Or that you haven't chosen the 'right' things. Or that you will attempt to do them and they won't work. Or you will give up.

Let me tell you now, you WILL fail with your bucket list!

You probably will never check it all off, and things won't happen the way you want them to some of the time. The thing about a bucket list is all of that doesn't matter. Actually a bucket list allows you to fail in an area of your life in which the consequences of failing aren't really that high.

I crossed off all my Top40 Bucket List items, but I also 'failed' on three of them. I said I would 'catch a fish' when in the end I went fishing but didn't catch anything. Note: wording of your bucket list items is important! Two other items were not done as I envisaged, either, but the point is that I attempted them.

Failure is a part of life. The only people who don't fail are the ones who don't try. Your true character is built not on whether you fail but on how and when you pick yourself back up again.

Maybe next time you will fail better! Do you know how many people care that I 'failed' at those three things? Zero. No one cares. Overall, people are impressed that I made an effort to do 40 bucket list items in one year. No one really cares about the details. Please look at failing as a good thing.

3. A Bucket List Makes You Fearless

Actually doing things on your bucket list does not automatically make you fearless. But as I mentioned earlier, the only way to beat fear is to move through it. Do the very thing that frightens you so that you are no longer scared of it. Know that the anticipation of the actual thing is far scarier than the thing is, so if you schedule it and do it, you reduce a lot of inner angst and conflict.

Stepping out of your comfort zone by doing things on a bucket list makes doing more things you find fearful—either on or off the bucket list—easier to do. Fear diminishes, and confidence and self-esteem improve, the more steps you take outside your comfort zone. This leads to personal growth, which is a key component to lifelong happiness, as will be explained in detail in a later chapter.

A surprising addition to the fearless benefit is that doing some of the things on my bucket list that terrified me the most (especially the tandem skydive) made other things seem less frightening. Since finishing the Top40 Bucket List I have seen a film, *The Cabin in the Woods* that I previously decided was too terrifying to watch. It was fine. I am looking forward to where my newfound courage takes me. I may one day be quite fine being in close quarters with a spider.

. . .

4. A Bucket List Gives You Control

This has been talked about in the previous chapter, but almost ironically, having a big list of things to do that are outside your comfort zone brings you a much-needed sense of control in life. You have certainty about variety and are therefore meeting two of your core needs in one go. This is very powerful.

A bucket list gives control via a few mechanisms: it brings about a sense of purpose in life, something to strive for, to accomplish. It gives your current work more meaning as it is not just paying the bills but helping you budget for the life you dreamed of. And a bucket list helps start or stop habits without using willpower. You decide to run a marathon, so you get in the habit of getting your running shoes on and going. You decide to snorkel at the Great Barrier Reef, so you start eating better to fit back into your swimsuit. You decide to take the family on that Disney Cruise next year, so you put aside some savings each week for it. That bigger goal makes the habit changes easier to bear.

The rest of the world may be going to hell in a hand basket, but this one thing, your personal bucket list, is a way of controlling exactly how you want to live before the zombie apocalypse actually happens.

5. A Bucket List Is Inspirational

The fact you are motivating yourself and directing energy to fun and challenging goals strikes a chord with many people. Your friends, family and especially your children will see that dreaming big is not only allowed but is also accessible with plans and goals.

Having a bucket list lets you become a better version of YOU.

Once you start checking items off, you not only get to feel successful and accomplished but others around you unwittingly learn valuable life lessons about failure, success and determination, among other things.

In a way, a bucket list could be considered an inspirational gift. You thought you were scribbling down a little list, but instead you were creating a magnificent legacy for now and for generations to come.

6. A Bucket List Shows Fun is Essential

Let's face it, in today's world where we all worship at the altar of busyness and distractedness, when is the last time you have had good clean fun? I don't mean finding happiness at the bottom of that glass of pinot or in the latest scroll or swipe, but in real life: backyard waterslide kind of fun. You need fun like you need work and family. You have just forgotten how essential it is.

If you have kids, embracing fun is even more critical. A bucket list will help you rediscover your carefree, playful and daring side. Aren't these attributes you would want your kids to see in you plus have in droves themselves? At the very least, a bucket list is a good way to stop boredom in its tracks. There are plenty of ideas for bucket list items to do as a family in Chapter Ten.

And if spending time with loved ones, being active and discovering new things aren't enough benefits, perhaps think of fun items on a bucket list another way. Many of us crave something sweet and think we will find it in the back of the pantry or fridge. But this craving for something sweet is not a nutritional need, it is a deep need for more light and laughter in your life. So do something nice for yourself that doesn't involve chocolate: create a bucket list and give yourself the chance to have some sweet and essential fun.

. . .

7. A BUCKET LIST FILLS YOUR CUP

Life today is filled with 'shoulds'. You should help others and should think about the environment and should live mindfully in your community. But this is very hard when you don't feel like you have much to give. You are often exhausted and overwhelmed with your life. You need your cup to be filled up before you can be generous without feeling resentful about it.

A bucket list is a perfect project to fill your cup. Doing something that fills you up inside and gives you a boost of joy spreads happiness to your loved ones and the world at large. You meet new people, appreciate other cultures and spend quality time with your kids. Positive emotions are useful and essential as they are linked to better health, longevity, productivity and social wellness.

As speaker and author, Lisa Nichols, eloquently describes it, fill your cup up so that it is overflowing onto the saucer and only then "serve" from your saucer.

Build a bucket list and create a win-win with the world.

OTHER BENEFITS OF A BUCKET LIST

Of course, a bucket list has a lot of other benefits not listed here in the areas of health, relationships and finances. It gets you off the sofa and outside in the fresh air that your grandmother always said was good for you. It provides the perfect reason to spend screen-free time with loved ones. It helps you to budget for the most important things you want to do with your hard-earned cash.

All the benefits of a bucket list, but especially the seven unexpected benefits above, hopefully get you amped up for writing your list. Because the next chapter is where the work begins. You WILL have 100 items on your bucket list by the end of Chapter Six.

6

WRITE YOUR BUCKET LIST

 'One day your life will flash before your eyes. Make sure it's worth watching.' – Gerard Way

YOU ARE READY!

The time has come to take action. By the end of this chapter you will have 100 items written down on the first draft of your bucket list. You may have come along for the motivational ride in the first few chapters, or you may be the 'show me the money' type of person who skipped straight here. Wherever you came from, if you have landed on this chapter YOU ARE READY.

Let's do this!

Yes, I said 100 bucket list items. Written down. Don't run away. This will be broken down into two easy steps. First a massive brainstorm of ideas and then a second stage that uses questions and prompts.

The most important thing to remember during this two-part exercise is to not only capture everything but also to really focus on and prioritize things YOU want to see, do, be and have. Once you start, you will find the ideas pour forth, so don't try and contain that fountain, but keep going back inside yourself and notice whether this is something YOU really want.

YET ANOTHER BENEFIT

One benefit not explicitly touched on in the previous chapter is that a bucket list helps you zero in on your true desires, focus in on what you really, really, really want in life and remind yourself of your long-held dreams. In other words, you tap into your own passions and end up knowing more about yourself. Getting a deeper understanding of the most important person in your life (you) is crucial to living a more fulfilling life.

We live in an age in which anything is possible and doable. You can book a trip into space if you want. But all the way through the exercises in this chapter, ask yourself if this is a 'HELL YEAH' bucket list item. As author and entrepreneur, Derek Sivers, states, "If you're not saying 'HELL YEAH!' about something, say 'no'".

Do you really want to bungy jump, or are you putting it down because it is a typical bucket list item? By all means, don't mute yourself at this point, get it down and you can remove it later. But capturing what you really want is a core part of this exercise.

This is meant to help you prioritize, streamline and get clear on your bucket list choices, not to overwhelm you. It may feel overwhelming at first, but in the end you will feel clearer about what you want. You will end up more in tune with yourself than you have ever been before.

Writing a bucket list is all about getting in touch with your truest, innermost desires, and creating massive personal intention to achieve them. You are only doing the first part here—tapping into you. Take the action part right out of the equation for now. Do not think about how you will actually check off the items.

STEP ONE: GET IT DOWN!

A key component to a bucket list is that it is written down. Writing it down makes it real, gets your thoughts in order and is a permanent record of your wants and dreams. You are more likely to achieve what you have written down. Do not skip this step. The writing part is very powerful.

Get it down!

What you need: something on which to write out your bucket list —a blank Word or other text document on your computer, or a large piece of paper or the back of an envelope. You are welcome to use the basic template in Appendix Three at the back of this book. Anything will do. Gather up some pens or colored markers as well, if needed. Then find something with which to time yourself for up to thirty minutes—a watch, phone timer or a giant hourglass, for example.

Don't do anything else in the time you set aside for this exercise. Don't check spellings of place names or what the capital city of a country is or if there is a surf school nearby. And for goodness sake, don't check the Internet for ideas, not at this point. You have a brain, so use it.

Now brainstorm, free write or mind map EVERYTHING you have always wanted to do, see, have, be, meet, etc. You KNOW in your heart what you want.

Have fun with this creative exercise. Be silly, invoke your curiosity, think outside the box. Think about fun things, challenging things, short-term activities, long-term pastimes, local places to visit and trips abroad. Think of your interests, hobbies, and passions. Dream big. Anything goes.

Get it down!

Write in short bullet points or long, descriptive paragraphs. Know that anything can be changed or deleted later. Don't worry if it seems more like a 'goal' than a bucket list item. The lines there are blurry, anyway. Don't worry that you don't have time or can't afford it or allow in any other negative thoughts. Don't worry if it seems too exotic, or conversely, too mundane. If it lights a fire in your belly, then it is perfect. Don't think it is not possible. If someone else in the world has done it, it is possible.

Get it down!

If it helps, write a 'NOT bucket list'. For instance, I will never do a bungy jump. Put that over to one corner of the page. Writing a NOT bucket list will help you clear the way for what you do want.

Finally, remember at this point that this does not have to look pretty. We will tidy it up later.

Aim for 100 items.

This may seem like a lot but it is not really. Remember the number of items on your bucket list doesn't really matter, but it is nice to have something to aim for.

Don't come back and do Step Two until you have got 100 items written down.

You have thirty minutes.

Go!

Step Two: Questions and Prompts

Questions and prompts help you to figure out more bucket list items and also focus on finding items more attuned to you. Using questions has been found to have a massive impact because if a question is asked, even if it is not spoken aloud, your mind is still compelled to answer it.

There are four general areas of questions. You don't have to answer all these questions. They are just there as prompts so you can add to your brand new, 100-item bucket list, or to refine it so it reflects YOU.

Santa's Knee Questions

These come in various forms, but overall they help you think like an excited five-year-old sitting on Santa's knee. There are no filters, no limits, no boundaries. Go wild, go crazy. Ask for the impossible. For example:

- What would you like if there were no financial limits?
- What would you do if you had unlimited time, money and resources?
- If you won a huge lottery, what would you do (after you paid off the mortgage)?
- If fear were not part of the equation what would you do?
- If you were given three wishes, what would you wish for (excluding world peace, of course)?
- What 'toy' or luxury item would you like to own or have, even for a day?

DEATHBED REGRETS QUESTIONS

These help you confront your own mortality. The traditional definition of a bucket list—a list of items to check off before you die—does that, but these really ram it home. For example:

- What would you like to have said about you in your eulogy?
- What do you absolutely HAVE to do before you die?
- What would be your biggest regret on your deathbed?
- What would you do, see, or have if you only had one day to live?
- What would you do, see, or have if you only had 30 days to live?
- What would you do, see, or have if you only had one year to live?
- What would you do, see, or have if you only had five years to live?

PASSIONS AND INTERESTS QUESTIONS

These help you to remember what you have always liked to do, or thought you would be good at but then decided that time, money or something else was in the way. These can be one-off things or longer-term hobbies. For example:

- What was your childhood dream to do, see, create?
- What have you always wanted to do that you felt like you didn't time for?
- What do you want to buy or do just to have fun?
- What would you do even without pay?

- What activity makes you lose track of time or gets you in a flow state?
- What has always been one of your biggest dreams in life?
- What would be a perfect day for you?

GET DOWN TO SPECIFICS QUESTIONS

The next chapter contains a lot of help to refine your bucket list and answer some of your burning questions, like "Do I just write 'India' or 'Visit the Taj Mahal'?". But to give you a taster, here are some questions that can help you think about your new bucket list in alternative ways.

- What would you HAVE—buy or own?
- What would you DO—see or create?
- Where would you like to visit or travel—countries, places, locations?
- What new foods do you want to taste?
- Who do you want to meet in person?
- What experiences do you want to have?
- What activities do you want to try at least once?
- What activities or skills do you want to learn or master?
- What adventures would get you out of your comfort zone?
- What would you do in different seasons of the year?
- Are there any special moments or scheduled events you want to witness?

YOU HAVE A BUCKET LIST!

This is the end of the main action-taking chapter. You have (at least) 100 bucket list items that make you smile, make your toes tingle and that make you want to jump out of bed in the morning.

They may be anything from silly little goals to epic adventures, crazy challenges or gentle achievements. The list is probably messy, in no particular order and you will have no idea how you would get even one item checked off, but you have your first draft bucket list!

If you haven't got 100 items yet, then don't worry; the next chapter helps you refine your personalized bucket list even more. It will also answer some of the questions that may have popped up during this two-part brainstorming and prompting exercise.

7

BUCKET LIST Q&A

 'Sometimes the questions are complicated and the answers are simple.' – Dr. Seuss

QUESTION AND ANSWER TIME

You now have 100 bucket list items scribbled down, and you are not sure what the heck you should do with the list. You are not even sure if it is 'right'. You are certainly not sure how you should begin crossing off the items, especially that super crazy 'fly into space' one. This chapter answers your burning questions about bucket lists and gives you some great tips so you can make your bucket list tidier AND more meaningful.

Q: I WAS HOPING FOR SOME IDEAS OR LISTS OF BUCKET LIST ITEMS. Can I look at the Internet now?

A: The brainstorm exercise purposely excluded use of the Internet, and there has been little reference to actual bucket list items up until this point so that you could tap into your own dreams and passions without being influenced by other people's ideas.

That said, there are some lists of bucket list items in the back of this book, including my Top40 Bucket List. And you can ask friends, use the Internet and get inspiration from all sorts of sources to add to your list. Now that you know how to tap into yourself, you will know upon seeing or hearing an idea if it is something you want to add to your list. Go check the Internet—I can't stop you from here!

Q: I AM NOT SURE IF THIS IS EVERYTHING I WANT TO DO. IS THIS A final list?

A: This bucket list is a first draft, a starting point. Your bucket list will evolve over the course of reading this book and then afterwards for the rest of your life. The most important thing is that you now have 100 items written down and that they are exciting and meaningful enough to you that you are willing to take action on them. That is it. The best bucket lists are simple and profound. Actually, I believe that the best things in life are both of those things, too.

Q: I HAVE WRITTEN SOME ITEMS DOWN, BUT I AM STILL NOT SURE IF they are what I really want—do I keep them on the list?

A: Short answer: YES. Like the first draft of anything, the first draft of your bucket list is not going to be your best work. You may not be sure if you want to take the item off because it is 'not really you' or because it suddenly seems too scary now that it is written down. Usually if it scares you, that is a good thing! So err on the side of caution and leave it on the list for now.

. . .

Q: How on earth am I going to get this entire list done?

A: You have time. You have the rest of your life! All you are doing at this stage is writing a list. Sure, scheduling items and putting deadlines in place plays a part—see Chapter Nine—but for now, don't worry.

> It is only a list of your most amazing dreams and deepest desires, nothing more(!).

One pro tip: stack or combine items. I wanted to attend an event, 'The World of Wearable Arts', which only happens in another city, Wellington. So I looked up other things to do in Wellington. I added 'Wellington Writers Walk' to my bucket list, and voila, two items that could be crossed off in the same weekend. Perhaps you want to learn to surf and do a meditation retreat? There are a number of places in Bali that offer both activities. Thinking 'stacking' when writing your list.

Please remember, you probably won't check off your entire bucket list in your lifetime, but that is not the point. Most people have no goals or only realistic goals. Be different. Set big, hairy audacious goals. Imagine a life in which half or a quarter or even one or two items are checked off—wouldn't it be far superior to the life you are currently living?

Q: I have written all this stuff down that I cannot afford or don't have time for, so where do I start?

A: The whole point of having a bucket list is to dream big but start small, and this will be detailed in Chapter Nine. For now, don't worry if you have written a big list of time consuming and expensive items. Writing an item down on your list is simply an acknowledgement that it is an item that you would like to tackle more than something that is not on your list.

Writing a bucket list is supposed to be fun, not stressful!

Q: I think my choices are too mundane. What if I don't want to do the travel or adventurous bucket list items?

A: Not everyone wants to ride in a hot air balloon over Cappadocia! Please do not worry if your choices don't seem exotic enough. A bucket list does not have to involve travel at all. You can take action on many items in your backyard. That is where I planted sunflower seeds and that is where I learned to juggle. Both are completely valid bucket list items.

Don't compare your bucket list to what you believe society thinks it should be. Most people will never have a bucket list, so who cares what they think, anyway? Modest goals you take action on are better than aspirational dreams you do nothing about.

One caveat to this—putting down items such as 'binge watch every episode of *Game of Thrones*' or 'get to the top level of a favorite computer game' is not really keeping with the essence of what a bucket list is about. Make your bucket list goals, however small, screen-free.

Q: I think my choices are too risky, how do I keep safe?

A: This is a repeat of the disclaimer from the front of this book:

This book is designed to give the reader (that means YOU – the exceptionally awesome person reading this!) some useful tips and ideas about how to create and put into action your personal bucket list. It has suggestions for bucket list items, but every reader is ultimately responsible for selecting the items for his or her bucket list.

Bucket list items may pose some risk. The author and publisher advise readers to take full responsibility for their safety and know their limits. What this means for YOU:

- Talk to a health professional before embarking on any increased physical activity.
- Make sure you have full and correct insurance (travel, health, etc.) whenever required.
- Use common sense to keep safe when traveling locally or abroad and research safety measures that are appropriate in other countries or regions.
- Make sure any equipment you use has been well-maintained.
- Choose reputable companies with the best safety records.
- Tell someone where you are going, what you are doing, and when you expect to be back.
- Choose bucket list items that are within your means financially or for which you are prepared to budget and save.
- Make responsible arrangements so that your work, family and other important areas of life remain in good condition while you pursue your bucket list.

Please, please, please do not choose irresponsible, destructive or illegal items for your bucket list.

The author and publisher accept no responsibility for any harm or loss resulting from your pursuit of the bucket list. Have fun, but keep safe.

. . .

Q: I don't have 100 items. Should I keep trying for a bigger list?

A: You have permission to use the Internet now, so feel free to add items. That said, the length of the bucket list is not important. Starting one is. Some people have a handful of items, some have thousands. I would personally recommend an absolute minimum of 25, but again, this is not supposed to be overwhelming.

If you have a written list of items that you are happy with, then don't worry about how many there are. Once you start checking some off, you will see how addictive a bucket list is and come up with more ideas effortlessly. Doing some of the items leads to other similar items, and your bucket list gains momentum organically.

Q: I am not sure if I have written my bucket list 'right', any suggestions?

A: Write a bucket list item in a way that gives you the most powerful impact or highlights the essential parts of the item.

One way to do this is to get as specific as possible. Create a descriptive story in your head or on paper about the item with the sensations you want to experience. On the actual list you can use action words to reduce this down to a phrase that gets the essence of the item across. For instance, 'soaking in an infinity pool with a cocktail in my hand and the warmth of the sun on my face as I watch a gorgeous sunset' gets reduced to 'swim in an infinity pool'.

Work out the main non-negotiables of the bucket list item. Even though I know I want to experience many things on a future trip to France, I have simply written 'France – try Champagne in the Champagne district, visit Monet's garden, ride a bike through tiny French villages. This gets me excited and highlights the essential parts that will be fleshed out when I take action on this item in a few years.

The only other limitation on a bucket list is that it is not a goals list. Your goals can be professional or family oriented. Although a bucket list may overlap across other fields, it is more about finding things you have never done before, that are memorable and that will give you a deep satisfaction in doing or achieving.

A bucket list would not normally include a work goal such as moving to a new position. But it could be in the professional realm, such as writing a business book. It is not a habit such as exercising three times per week, but it could be a physical challenge such as winning a tennis tournament. It is not a resolution such as 'always be kind', but it could be a charitable challenge such as perform five random acts of kindness in a day.

If you are not sure if the item is a 'true' bucket list item or a life goal, don't worry. The fact that you have written it down means that, regardless of where it sits, it is more likely to happen. Some people would say, for instance, 'buying a house' is not a bucket list item but 'building a house' is. Bottom line is, it does not matter one iota. Get it down!

Q: THIS BUCKET LIST IS A MESS, IT IS NOT PRIORITIZED, AND I DON'T know where to start. Help!

A: This is your first draft bucket list. It is supposed to look messy. The next chapter will give you some ideas on how to organize and categorize your bucket list. This is completely optional, so feel free to skip that chapter if you are happy with how your list looks.

Q&A Delay

Remember, just like the objections chapter, these questions are partly a delay attempt by your fearful mind to make you think you don't want to have a bucket list. Your thoughts could lead you to believe that writing down things that you may never get to do is pointless. But denying yourself the dream of swimming in infinity pools or cycling through tiny French villages is just as intolerable.

A bucket list is fun, but it takes time and effort and so it is hard work. Not having a bucket list, a chance to dream, is a painful, unsatisfactory and hard way to live. Choose your hard.

If you still want to delay taking action on your bucket list, or if you really want to tidy it up and get a bit more clarity around all the items, then the next chapter on categories and organization is for you. If you want to leap into actually checking off your first item, then skip to Chapter Nine.

8

ORGANIZE YOUR BUCKET LIST

 'A place for everything and everything in its place.' –
Benjamin Franklin

A Major Achievement

Congratulations on your brand new written down bucket list!
Feel proud, as most people never write their bucket lists down.
Feel excited as you are connecting into long-held dreams. And
feel positive as you are focusing on things you really want to do.

This chapter is completely optional. You definitely do not have to
organize your list in any way. You can just have a straight list that
is in no particular order. Just writing a list is a major achievement.
Pat yourself on the back and move on to the next chapter. But if
you like the idea of organizing your list into common areas, this
chapter is for you.

These ideas to categorize your bucket list are meant to be a help,
not a hindrance. Please don't let this chapter overwhelm you as

you are not sure what category to place items in or you haven't thought of items in a particular category. You don't need items in every category! One or two categories may be really long and others have only a handful of items. If re-organizing your list prompts you to think of more items, change items or even remove items, it is actually a good extra function of categorization.

Think of this chapter as an extra tool that can make your bucket list better. It is simply a way to structure your list in a way that may help it to make more sense to you. But if you don't want to take on the suggestions, please leave this tool in the toolbox for now.

Most importantly, don't let the suggestions here distract you from the goal of checking off items. Spend a little time organizing your bucket list and then move on to the next chapter. That is where the real magic happens.

Your Choice

There are a number of ways to categorize your bucket list. There are a few different approaches outlined below plus a suggested template. Most websites on bucket lists also have good category ideas, especially www.bucketlist.org. There is a list of websites in the References section at the end of the book.

The first way to organize your list is to go through the items and find any patterns or themes in them that naturally group them together. You can be quite general or specific here. You could include subcategories. You may want to rank the items or organize them along a time continuum. Of course, there will likely be crossover between categories, but just try to slot them into one place. For example, 'Dining at the top of the Eiffel Tower'—is that 'Travel' or 'Food' related? Whatever makes the most sense to you.

Note that alongside the different category templates, there will be a few examples of bucket list items. Feel free to add them to your bucket list if they speak to you.

Possible Category Templates

You could organize your list with some sort of time reference. For example, split items into the different seasons. Another way is to distinguish 'event specific' versus 'anytime' items. Some items, like concerts and festivals, will only be possible on specific dates and some, like indoor rock climbing, can be scheduled year-round. Or you could rank items in relation to when you want to do them, such as this month, this year, the next two years, five years, ten years, etc.

You may notice that items easily fall into the different senses. Or perhaps separate challenges into mental versus physical. For instance, solve a Rubik's cube versus do a triathlon. Travel items could be grouped into local, national and international categories.

Bucket list items could be spaced on a continuum from try out once to master a skill, leisurely to more adventurous or cheaper to expensive. For example:

- Try out versus master: try playing a ukulele, learn the guitar, play in a rock band
- Leisurely to more adventurous: fly in a seaplane, fly in an aerobatic plane, fly in a fighter jet
- Cheaper to more expensive: ride on a hired tandem bike, do a tandem skydive

Another way to view your bucket list is to tag what you would like to do by yourself versus with others—partners, kids and friends. More on this in Chapter Ten.

SUGGESTED CATEGORY TEMPLATE

My top favorite category template is an acronym that spells 'BUCKET'. Here it is:

B – Buy
U – Undertakings
C – Create
K – Kindness
E – Experiences
T – Travel

This is what the categories mean:

B – Buy – Material items you want to buy or own
U – Undertakings – Things to learn or master, or challenges you want to do
C – Create – Stuff you want to make or build or that will use your creativity
K – Kindness – Items with a charitable focus or kind acts for others
E – Experiences – Adventurous pursuits, fun activities or exciting experiences
T – Travel – Anything travel and tourism related

Here is the 'BUCKET' category system using examples from my Top40 Bucket List:

B – Buy- Hanging 'egg' chair

U – Undertakings- Write a novel in a month
C – Create- Plant and grow sunflowers
K – Kindness- N/A
E – Experiences- Ride on a jet ski, try curling
T – Travel- Fly to Queenstown for a burger

Here is the 'BUCKET' category system using other examples:

B – Buy- A vintage airplane, stamp collection
U – Undertakings- Learn to tango, learn Spanish
C – Create- Knit a scarf, write a song
K – Kindness- Give blood, work in a soup kitchen for a day
E – Experiences- Go on a trapeze, cuddle a lion cub
T – Travel- Raft the Grand Canyon, visit Hawaii

As you see from the examples above, you do not have to place items in every category. I purposely didn't put any charity or community focused items on my Top40 Bucket List as I give in other ways. You will also notice that it is sometimes still hard to classify items. Fly to Queenstown for a burger. Is that more 'Travel' or 'Experiences'? Ultimately, any classification is at your discretion.

Even though there are some downsides to this particular template, I love this as it is easy to remember, it is wide enough to capture almost every bucket list item imaginable, and it organizes items into intuitively decipherable categories. Of course, there may be some that don't easily fall into a one of the spots or could be cross categorized, but that will occur with any attempt to structure your bucket list.

ADDITIONAL TRAVEL CATEGORY TEMPLATE

Depending on how many travel related items you have on your bucket list, you may want to subcategorize the 'Travel' category. I didn't need to do this with my Top40 Bucket List as I only had a few travel items. However, I have created a handy template that you are welcome to use. And, of course, it is an acronym of the word 'TRAVEL:

T – Transport- Use of planes, trains, bikes, cruise ships, etc.
R – Restaurants and Food- Restaurants, food or drink from places or cultures
A – Activities and Adventure- Fun or exciting endeavors
V – Visit- Places to visit and sightsee
E – Experiences and Events- Booked experiences or date specific events
L – Lodging- Accommodation and places to stay

Here are some examples of items that fall into the 'TRAVEL' template:

T – Transport- Ride on the Orient Express, drive Route 66
R – Restaurants and Food- Eat at a Michelin star restaurant, try fried crickets
A – Activities and Adventure- Dogsled in Alaska, swim with whales in Tonga
V – Visit- Go to the Galapagos Islands, see Niagara Falls
E – Experiences and Events- Attend Burning Man festival, visit Dollywood
L – Lodging- Stay at the Ice Hotel, stay in a Scottish castle

Notice that some items are specific to a place and other ideas can happen in different parts of the world. Again, it may be hard to choose which category an item falls into. Deciding what is an 'Adventure', what is a 'Visit' and what is an 'Experience' may be difficult at times. Is going to Dollywood an adventure, a visit or an experience? Just go with your gut and place it based on your first instinctive decision.

In Appendix Two there are a few more examples of bucket list items that use the 'BUCKET' and 'TRAVEL' category templates to give you an even better understanding of categorization.

Categorize Quickly and Move On

This chapter is a way to make your bucket list more manageable so you don't feel overloaded with 100 items in a long list. If doing this does overwhelm you, then stop! Keep your file just as it is.

But if you have found a category system that works for you or you are using the 'BUCKET' and 'TRAVEL' templates, then quickly rewrite your list.

In either case, the most important step is to move onto the next chapter. This is where you get to finally take action on that first bucket list item.

9

CHECK OFF THE FIRST BUCKET LIST ITEM

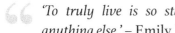 *'To truly live is so startling it leaves little time for anything else.'* – Emily Dickinson

IT IS ACTION TIME

You have a bucket list of at least 25 and preferably 100 (or even more) items. It may be in categories or simply be a straight list. You are happy with the list, it feels like 'you', and it is complete for now.

This chapter is about how to get your list into a format that you will read on a regular basis and then put into action. By the end of this chapter you will have done at least one item on your list. It is very important to get the feeling of achievement that comes with actually checking a bucket list item off, as that creates a drive to do more of the items.

It's time to stop 'listing' and start living!

Display and Read Your Bucket List

If your bucket list has been done with pen and paper, I recommend creating a digital version of the list, whether in a Word document, typed in an email to yourself or in a notes app on your phone, just so you have another copy of it somewhere.

Make sure you have your first, finalized version of your bucket list somewhere you have easy access to it and see it every day. Use the pen and paper version or print it out and stick it to your wall, on the fridge, on the bathroom mirror, or for those who are more private, inside the door to your wardrobe. Or tuck it into a journal you write in regularly.

If you have an electronic Word document or PDF of your bucket list, then place that document on your computer desktop, or add it into your notes or books apps on your phone.

Some of you who are more public may want to share your bucket list on your favorite social media feed, on Pinterest or on your own blog. Sharing it and getting others involved keeps you even more accountable, but it may not be for everyone. More on this soon.

A fun but completely optional way to display your bucket list is to create a 'vision board' from it. A vision board is any sort of board on which you display images that represent your bucket list items —what you want to do, see and have in life.

Create one the old-fashioned way out of cut outs from magazines stuck to a big piece of paper or cardboard. Or combine some pictures into an online board on Pinterest or elsewhere.

An extra cool idea is to take a photo of your written bucket list or its physical vision board and upload it so it becomes your computer screen saver or wallpaper on your phone.

Choose to display your bucket list in a way that reflects you. Don't spend days and days on this point as it can easily turn into a procrastination attempt. The point is to not forget your bucket list. Look at it, refer to it and read it often. It will become more real the more you review it and then you are more likely to take action with it.

SCHEDULE YOUR DREAMS

So far, you have been asked to dream big. Now it is time to schedule your dreams. You have a bucket list somewhere handy. Now scan through the list and find TWO items you can put in your diary, calendar or online scheduling program. How you schedule things, on a digital system or physically written down, is not important. What is important is getting them in the diary.

Choose the FIRST item that you can check off quickly. Think LOW COST or LOCAL or LITTLE TIME. As part of the Top40 Bucket List, I decided to try curling. I found a local ice-skating rink and went to their Sunday night one-hour long tryout session for $10. It was kind of fun and kind of a challenge and I bruised my knee badly, but that is not the point. I checked off that bucket list item relatively easily as it was low cost, local and took little time.

Choose a SECOND item that will take some planning in terms of expense, research or resources required. Around the same time I checked off 'try curling' from my bucket list, I started planning the trip to Wellington for 'The World of Wearable Arts' event that was happening later in the year. I looked up tickets, airfares and accommodation and started booking them.

It doesn't matter what day or time you put the item in, or whether you think you will be able to do it; just scheduling it gives it a lot of power, almost a life of its own. If you have to reschedule it, fine. But it will always be in your diary until you have taken action on it.

WHY STARTING SMALL WORKS

The way to start your bucket list is to start small. Check one 'easy win' item off and do little things (look up flights, etc.) on the bigger things.

This low-hanging fruit starts building your 'bucket list action taker' muscle. The happy feeling of checking things off, even the small things, makes you feel like your bucket list is achievable. By DOING, you change your beliefs on what you think you can do. This creates excitement, a fire in your belly, a reason to spring out of bed in the morning.

You may have thought there was a one-way street between thought and behavior. You smile because you are happy. But that is not always the case. Think about the times you make yourself smile even when you are not feeling that happy. Does your body make you think you are a bit happier simply by smiling?

The same analogy applies to taking action on your bucket list. Doing one thing, anything at all, interrupts your normal thought patterns and makes you think that these previously impossible things are now possible. Utilize the power of DOING and see how much your beliefs around acting on your long-held dreams change.

When I wrote out my Top40 Bucket List, there were a number of LOW COST or LOCAL or LITTLE TIME items. I did many of these in the first few months of the year. It gave me a handful of small successes and made me think checking off the entire 40 items in a year would be achievable.

Six items I did early on: planting sunflower seeds, trying a gourmet ice-cream place, starting a memory jar with my four-year-old, trying stand up paddle boarding, trying a rosé wine ice-block and trying curling cost less than $50 in total. All together they gave me a huge boost in confidence that I could tackle some of the more daunting and expensive items such as a hot air balloon ride and a tandem sky dive.

Accountability

Writing a bucket list, reading it and even scheduling items may not be enough to actually do them. It can be a good idea to add some accountability to your bucket list.

Now, some of you may not want to tell the world about your deepest desires, and that is perfectly valid. You may be worried that others will tell you that what you want to do is impossible. You may not want to set yourself up to fail in public. And you may not want people to think you are being selfish or crazy. As we have discussed, most people will never attempt to have a bucket list so their reactions do not matter. However, keep your bucket list private for now if that feels right for you.

If you want to go public it is super easy these days. Paste your bucket list online everywhere and tell your friends about it. Update your Facebook, Instagram or Pinterest presence with photos of your bucket list wins. Ask your friends and family to join you in some of the experiences you want to do. And don't be afraid to ask for their help to check off items.

When I decided on my wacky endeavor to do 40 bucket list items in a year, I asked friends for their suggestions. Some ideas were exactly what I would like to do, but they had to go on a long-term bucket list due to financial or logistic constraints.

One thing I really wanted to do but had no idea if it was possible was to fly an hour and a half to Queenstown to eat a burger from an infamous burger joint called FergBurger, which serves such amazing burgers that it always has a line of hungry people snaking down the block. It ended up making the Top40 cut thanks to two friends. One friend was happy to come with me on the adventure and had air points to use up, and another friend happened to have just moved to Queenstown and could pick us up from the airport and take us to the burger place. This made it both financially and logistically possible. In the fresh air of Queenstown, under the stunning vista of the surrounding mountains, that was, without doubt, the best burger I have ever eaten.

Use Deadlines

Another way to stay accountable, if only to yourself, is to create deadlines. Some items will naturally have limited times. For instance, if you want to see a particular artist in concert, go to a specific festival or see a seasonal or natural wonder like the Northern Lights or an eclipse.

Sometimes, however, deadlines are completely artificial but are strong enough to be an inspiration. I set a goal to check 40 things off my bucket list during the calendar year of 2016. I jumped out of a plane on the 30th of December 2016, one day before my deadline. Yes, it was self-imposed. And no one else would care if I jumped out on the 1st of January 2017. But I would. As I had completed the rest of the list and there was a deadline looming, completing the jump became more important than the fear.

Referring to your bucket list regularly, scheduling items, starting small, telling people your intentions and using deadlines are fantastic ways to make your bucket list happen. Together they create an enormously powerful force that makes it almost impossible not to take action.

ACTION TIME: PICK OUT ONE ITEM FROM YOUR BUCKET LIST that you can do in the next week. Think LOW COST or LOCAL or LITTLE TIME (or all three). Get excited, get ready and get it done.

10

BUCKET LISTS WITH FAMILY AND FRIENDS

 'Life isn't about waiting for the storm to pass; it's about learning to dance in the rain.' – Vivian Greene

SHARING IS CARING

Up until now you will be forgiven for thinking that creating a bucket list is a very individual endeavor. This book has focused on the bucket list you create being personal and related to your dreams and passions. The items are things you want to do, regardless of whether anyone else is interested.

But where is the fun in that? There is nowhere near as much joy in completing your bucket list items by yourself, as there is in including others.

You may object to this, as it is not their bucket list. And yes, you are right. But a large portion of the population will never create their own bucket lists. Most people are usually quite happy to hop on board when someone is planning something fun or exciting. If you show yourself as a leader in this area, you are likely to find someone you know who will join you when you embark on your next crazy idea.

Although I was happy to do all of my Top40 Bucket List items on my own, in the end I only did nine of the 40 by myself. From stand up paddle boarding, to curling, to even that daunting tandem skydive, I had a friend who was happy to join me. In the case of 'Drunk Shopping', which was officially my 40th birthday celebration, I had a whole bunch of friends who were happy to have a few glasses of wine over lunch and then go shopping. So. Much. Fun!

Partners

If you have a special someone in your life, creating a bucket list is a perfect way to spend quality time with him or her. Your loved one can tag along on your bucket list ideas, or—even better—you can both create a list and decide on your favorite ideas that you would like to do together.

Other than the obvious of not being alone, there are a ton of benefits of marking off bucket list items with your other half. Doing things together strengthens a relationship, as there are usually positive memories associated with the task. You can reminisce with your partner about the time you visited Tuscany and made pasta from scratch or kissed under that waterfall you hiked to last summer.

If you like to do more adventurous things together, then it has been shown in dating experiments that anything that makes the heart race increases attractiveness between couples. There is a theory that even though the heart is racing due to the activity, the mind can easily believe it is due to the allure of the other person. And in other studies, it has been proven that couples in long-term relationships feel more attracted to each other when they regularly engage in novel and exciting activities that involve working together to achieve a goal, for example, building a tree house together.

Most things on a bucket list are adaptable for two people, but some ideas are especially suitable for couples. Great ideas specifically for twosomes include doing a tandem bike ride together, dance lessons, mastering your chess game, trying indoor rock climbing, or anything that seems romantic like a couples massage, sunset watching or dinner at a Michelin star restaurant.

CHILDREN

No matter how old your children are, a bucket list can bring about unforgettable experiences and cherished family memories. Again, like couples, you could bring the kids along for the ride on your own bucket list or invite them to think of items and create a family list. Kids, once prompted, are very good at this exercise. They will have a wish list a mile long before you know it.

Whichever way you choose to do this depends on how old your kids are and whether they are enthusiastic about your ideas already. But just making a family bucket list together—before you check anything off—is helpful for connecting on a higher level with your tiny humans.

There are lots of benefits when the whole family is involved with checking off a bucket list. Your kids gain important life skills such as persistence, making decisions and tackling risk in a controlled environment with a parent around. They learn to make goals and achieve them, and they grow less fearful and more confident as a result. Just like you, they have to move away from their usual comfort zones and add some variety and adventure into their young lives. If travel outside of your local area is involved, they may get a better understanding of other cultures and gain empathy for different people they meet.

Also, you bond more with your kids as you share common fears, struggles and obstacles. Even if you end up doing the actual item by yourself (like running a marathon, for example), they can come with you on training runs and cheer from the sidelines on the big day. And if they are fully involved (like mastering a card trick or building a go-cart together), this can only enhance the strong relationship you already have.

> If nothing else, it gets your kids and you off screens and into real life—and everyone can agree that that is a wonderful thing.

ONE BUCKET LIST IDEA SPECIFICALLY DESIGNED WITH KIDS IN MIND is creating a memory jar. A memory jar is simply any jar or box that gets filled up with little notes about fun family times you have done together. So on your bucket list you can write 'create a memory jar' and when you complete items from your bucket list, you can write a little note or draw a picture, or keep the ticket stub, etc., and add it to the jar.

This is kind of meta, but also cheap and easy, plus it helps your children savor the experience even more. More about savoring in the next chapter as a good way of enhancing your bucket list experience. Similar to the memory jar idea, you can create a time capsule or a treasure chest as a family.

Other (mostly very low cost) ideas with kids include playing a round of disc (Frisbee) golf, trying to catch a fish (e.g.: from a wharf), learning to juggle, performing a magic trick, making a pottery bowl, knitting a scarf, folding origami into a special design, going ice-skating, planting a tree or putting a message in a bottle and throwing it out to sea together.

This is just the tip of the iceberg to give a flavor of cheap, cool things that will bring you together as a family, keep the kids off the screens, and give you all positive memories that will last a lifetime.

FRIENDS

As already noted, a bucket list item is usually enhanced with a friend or two joining you. I know I wouldn't have enjoyed the hot air balloon ride or the tandem skydive as much if it weren't for a brave friend, in each of the experiences, who said that they were keen to join me.

But the power of bucket lists can really be seen if a big group of you gets together and does something. If you want to build a house for charity, for example, then this is much better when you can rope in a whole bunch of buddies who can help. Sharing the joy of achieving a big goal makes it even better.

Other bucket list ideas that really lend themselves to bigger groups or require some help and support include: throwing a surprise party, attempting to break a Guinness World Record, going to a music festival or creating a flash mob. And if you have ever wanted to get hold of one of those enormous bottles of champagne so you could shower it everywhere, it is much better if you have some friends around who have 'get soaked with champagne' on their bucket lists.

Really, almost every bucket list item you can imagine with the possible exception of learning to ride a unicycle (but even then a steady hand from another person may be useful) is better with someone else. So share your bucket list with your friends and family. You may be surprised to find out that some latent dreams that your nearest and dearest have been harboring are already on your bucket list, and you are a catalyst for them finally taking action.

Checking off your bucket list with friends and family is a great way to supercharge it, to enhance the positive attributes of it. But it is not the only way. The next chapter shows how you can get the most out of your bucket list.

11

SUPERCHARGE YOUR BUCKET LIST

 'It's kind of fun to do the impossible.' – Walt Disney

MAGNIFY YOUR HAPPINESS

You may be feeling fairly sorted and settled on your bucket list, especially now that you have checked off at least one thing. This is fun! This is doable! This is making me feel awesome! Now, in this penultimate chapter, you have the option of making your bucket list even more amazing by directly connecting it to proven drivers for happiness.

If you are content with how your bucket list is tracking right now, feel free to disregard this chapter. However, all these ideas magnify the happiness that you can extract from your bucket list, so they are worth noting. Have a quick peek at the following five suggestions and see if any resonate with you.

. . .

1. Create a Challenge Around Your Bucket List

As I have been describing all the way through this book, in 2016, the year I turned 40, I wrote down 40 things I wanted to do, see, experience or have within the 12 months from January to December. I called this my 'Top40 Bucket List'. To cut a long story short—yes—I did take action on every single Top40 bucket list item and managed to complete them in the 12 months, with just a day to spare when I jumped out of a plane on the 30th of December 2016.

It was hard work! I definitely made some mistakes and had some issues. Technically, three items were not done properly, but I did at least try them or start them. I should have done some more items earlier in the year over summertime instead of leaving them right to the end. And by procrastinating on the tandem skydive, even though it was a spectacular way to finish of the Top40, I let it create a lot of fear in my mind. I should have gotten it done earlier.

I sure wish I'd had a book just like this one to refer to when I decided to embark on this crazy challenge.

But even though it was hard, it was without doubt one of the best experiences of my entire life. Up there with my wedding and the birth of my children. Setting a 'BHAG' – a big, hairy, audacious goal, and then actually achieving it makes me feel proud, improves my self-esteem and makes me believe I can be a better person.

> By exceeding what I thought my potential was, by seeing
> that I was only limited by my own beliefs, I feel like I am
> in an excellent position to tackle further challenges and
> smash through fears.

It may seem like creating a bucket list is enough of a challenge, but if you amp it up—do so many items in a year, or before you turn a certain age, or add items that you are very fearful of or that really challenge and stretch you—I guarantee you will feel even more happy and fulfilled.

Trying to mark off bucket list items is hard. Adding a crazy challenge to your bucket list project that will make you feel more fulfilled and happy but also increases the risk of failure is hard. Choose your hard.

2. BE GRATEFUL

Being grateful creates awareness of the good in your life. Gratitude studies have shown that an appreciation practice is associated with being more enthusiastic about life, being interested in the community, being kinder to others and getting better sleep, among a myriad of other positive outcomes.

Being thankful for knowing you can create a bucket list, feeling appreciative when writing down some of your dreams and then feeling gratitude when you check off some of the items can enhance your bucket list experience tremendously.

There is a deceptively simple but powerful exercise called 'Three Good Things'. Use it whenever you are taking action on your bucket list and multiply your happiness. You can also do this exercise at the end of the day about anything in your life, not just your bucket list, as a daily gratitude practice.

Three Good Things:

1. List ONE good or happy thing from your day.
2. Write it down, tell your partner or speak the answer out loud to yourself.

3. Ask yourself WHY it happened—what was it about YOU (your character, personality, traits, strengths, qualities or skills, etc.) that helped it to occur.
4. Take a few moments to feel good about yourself—SAVOR that positive feeling.
5. Do this whole exercise again for TWO more things if you have time.

For example, I looked up the best and most scenic places to safely bicycle around in France today. This helped me take one step towards my future trip to France that I wrote down on my bucket list. Feeling excited about planning this trip will make it easy for me to start saving for it.

It is not the good thing that is important but the connection to you, that third step, that is the supercharging mechanism. Step three focuses on your role in creating that good thing and gets you thinking about specific positive traits in YOU that contributed to the happy moment.

Over time you see that you have control over creating these happy experiences, and your positive outlook starts to be imbedded in your identity. So you get to feed your need for certainty and transform your identity, two of the most powerful drivers of your life. The savoring step simply locks in all the goodness from the whole exercise.

3. SAVOR THE EXPERIENCE

Positive psychologists, researchers whose focus is happiness and other positive emotional states, describe three tiers to happiness: living a pleasurable life, a good life and a meaningful life. All three of these tiers can be applied to bucket lists.

Check back at those 'deathbed regret' questions that prompted you to think of bucket list items. They asked what you would do, see or have with one day, 30 days, one year or five years to live. Very loosely, the shorter time periods can correspond to a pleasurable life and the longer ones to a good or meaningful life.

One criticism of a bucket list is that is just a pleasant distraction from normal life. And perhaps it is. But even if you choose just 'pleasurable' activities and not ones that are related to what positive psychologists call a 'good' or 'meaningful' life, your bucket list items will still serve a greater purpose than being a frivolous diversion.

But only if you **savor** them. Savoring, or its synonyms, luxuriating, reveling, marveling, relishing or basking are easy methods of finding pleasure in everyday moments.

So while you are in the middle of your bucket list item, really take it in, be completely mindful of the moment, even for a few seconds. Let your brain absorb and relish in this positive activity. Try to be fully present.

If you forget at the time, you can savor an experience you have not done yet. In fact, one of the main reasons to write a bucket list is to get you excited about doing the things on it. In other words, you can still live a pleasurable life even if you are future oriented. Studies have proven that planning, researching and looking forward to experiences creates almost as much happiness as the experience itself. This seems to only apply to experiences and not material purchases. Sometimes the best laid plans may have to be cancelled last minute, but that doesn't necessarily counter the days, weeks or months of happy anticipation you already had.

Probably the best way to savor your bucket list is to create ways to remember all the tasks you have completed. You can bask in the past. You can take photos of each one and put them in a special

'Bucket List Album' (digital or physical). You can share what you did with others. Or you can create a box of keepsakes or a memory jar as described previously. If your bucket list involves a lot of travel, perhaps getting a world map and dotting it with pins of places you have been to is a good way to savor your experiences. There are many options, but please find some way to congratulate yourself and celebrate every single item.

4. LINK YOUR BUCKET LIST ITEMS TO YOUR STRENGTHS

Although the pleasures in life—especially if you are mindful of them—will give you a pleasurable life, there is another level that gives you 'a good life'. This is where you use your strengths and abilities to work towards something, create something or improve yourself.

Checking off a bucket list is a perfect opportunity to try something new, challenge yourself with a task or attempt to master something. In other words, it enables you to use your strengths and abilities to attain 'a good life'. Try to ensure you have at least a few items that involve personal effort. For example, training to run a marathon, learning a new language or reconditioning an old classic car.

If you want mostly fun and pleasurable activities on your bucket list, then by all means focus on that first tier of happiness. No judgment here! There is no mandate to add in these pursuits that may not make you feel good at first, but help you grow as a person. But once you have satiated yourself on the pleasures in life, consider adding in a couple of challenges to your bucket list. You may be surprised about how fulfilled they make you feel.

When I participated in National Novel Writing Month (NaNoWriMo) as part of my Top40 Bucket List, writing 50,000 words (equivalent of a 200-page book) in a month seemed daunting. It was, surprisingly, a massive happiness boost as the challenge pushed me to enhance my existing writing skills, tap into my creativity and overall grow as a person. It doesn't matter that the silly romance novel I wrote is sitting in the proverbial bottom drawer and is unlikely to be published, the challenge in itself was extremely rewarding.

Remember back in Chapter Four when the need for growth was discussed as a critical need that many people diminish as other needs take priority? Adding challenges to your bucket list that require you to develop existing abilities or master new skills fulfills this deep need for growth in a positive way.

5. Bring More Meaning to Your Bucket List

A bucket list improves your life, makes you happier and therefore contributes to a better world. But for some of you, this still won't be enough of a reason to create one. You need something more.

The ultimate aim is not only to live a pleasurable life or good life but a **meaningful** life. You attain a meaningful life from a connection to a wider cause. In other words, from fulfilling your need for contribution. The positive psychologists and personal development gurus have intersected here again, both with an emphasis on giving.

You certainly do not have to add any item onto your bucket list that involves charitable work, but for some, this will add a layer of meaning to their bucket list. In fact, I don't recommend it at all unless you feel like you have something to give. And the best way to do that is to feel fulfilled yourself before you give, so do some of your own personal dream items from your bucket list first.

Once you have checked off a few 'fill your own cup' items, feel free to add and take action on items such as 'work in a soup kitchen for a day' or 'bake cupcakes for the local rest home', or 'help build a school in a developing country'.

A fun way to gain meaning from your bucket list is to add an item such as 'do five random acts of kindness in one day' or 'do one random act of kindness per day for a month'. You can get lots of ideas from randomactsofkindness.org. For instance, offer a glass of water to the package delivery person, leave some extra coins in the parking meter or send a friend a bunch of flowers out of the blue. It has been proven that doing five acts of kindness in a single day gives a significant boost to happiness—maybe a new idea to try out as a part of a family bucket list?

And yes, helping others to achieve their bucket list dreams is an extremely satisfying way to add more meaning to your bucket list. Ask people what would be their ultimate dreams and help them to step out of their comfort zones.

Be a leader, be a friend.

Supercharging Options

These high-level suggestions to supercharge your bucket list are all optional. Just reading this book and writing out some bucket list items may be enough for you right now.

Please remember to read this chapter when you are a little further along in your bucket list project. It may prompt you to add a challenge, remember to feel gratitude, savor your experiences, or add items that will extend you as a person or bring even more meaning into your life.

Next, the final chapter is a wrap up of the main take home points of this book.

12

BUCKET LIST WRAP UP

 'To live is the rarest thing of all. Most people exist, that is all. – Oscar Wilde

THE SIX HUMAN NEEDS (AGAIN)

Look at what you have accomplished with reading this book— you not only have a bucket list of 100 items that reflects your deepest desires and long-held dreams, but you have checked off one or more items on it already.

Many, many people in this world cannot fathom the amazing feeling you can invoke from writing down a goal and then taking action to achieve it. Not only do you now know what that feeling is like, you also know exactly how to get it back again, over and over, by checking off more bucket list items.

Remember that feeling of certainty we all crave at the deepest level? As you can now see, ironically you can get that exact feeling—feeling secure in yourself because you are in charge of your life—by increasing the level of variety in your life. That is, by meeting your need for certainty, through taking action systematically on your bucket list, you also get to meet one of your other main needs, the need for variety.

All of your other needs are also met through writing down a personalized bucket list and taking action on it. You meet your need for significance, as you know most people never attempt to write a bucket list and even fewer take action with it. You also meet your need for love as you often attain your bucket list items with your family and friends and so strengthen your relationships with them. And of course, you learn about yourself and set challenges to master skills and so meet your need for growth. Plus, if you add a few community-minded ventures onto your list you can meet your need for contribution. What other tool can help meet so many needs—in a positive way—at the same time?

A Mere Tool

A bucket list is not just a nice thing to have; it is a necessary part of a satisfying life, as shown by the fact that it meets all your deepest human needs.

But it is still only a tool.

In fact, although this whole book has been about creating and taking action on your bucket list, the main message is to get you to focus and decide what you really want in life. The bucket list is simply an instrument to help you understand yourself better, reconnect with your innermost desires and take action in spite of the fear.

This bucket list book has hopefully shown you that if you step out of your comfort zone to try something new, the world will not end.

You get to dance with fear instead of cowering from it.

Sure, you may not succeed, but trying and failing is always better than not trying because of the fear.

It is also about connecting with others. Getting you to do things out in the world that make you interact with other cultures and societies. Enabling you to simply have fun and complete challenges with loved ones—partners, kids, family and friends. No other factor in positive psychology research has been linked to increased happiness more than good, close, loving relationships, and a bucket list is a great facilitator in this regard.

Use this bucket list book, your own bucket list and your rediscovered ability to take action, to design the life you want, to have fun, to understand yourself better and to connect with others.

Isn't that what life is all about?

SIMPLE YET POWERFUL

You don't have to share your bucket list with anyone, and you don't have to invite friends and family to do it with you. Even if you keep your bucket list private, your loved ones will see a change in you. They will notice that you have more of a spring in your step as you focus on what you want, that you have a newfound zest for life and seem lighter and happier overall.

A good, well-written bucket list captures what you really want in life. In doing so, it will create an excitement deep in your soul that will easily lead you to living life to the fullest. It is an effortless way to invite energy and enthusiasm back into your life.

It is truly astounding that a simple list of goals and dreams can be the catalyst for a more fulfilling life. That all it takes to avoid those deathbed regrets is to tap into what you want and do something about it. But now that you have seen it and felt it.

You know deep down how powerful a bucket list can be.

The most important thing to remember with a bucket list is not to let it stagnate. Keep looking at it, adding to it, changing it, and most importantly, checking items off of it. Don't be afraid to be spontaneous and be flexible. This is meant to be a long-term practice that will turn into a habit and be part of your lifestyle. The most important thing is to take action. Live.

Go and take a look at your bucket list right now and find another thing you can take action on before you close this book. Enquire about that salsa dancing class, ask for some vacation time for that multi-day hike or book in that Michelin star restaurant at its next available slot. Plant those sunflower seeds today.

It doesn't matter what you do, just that you do something.

APPENDIX ONE - MY TOP40 BUCKET LIST

This is the approximate order in which I ended up checking off items.

1. Plant and grow sunflowers
2. Start a memory jar with Dylan
3. Eat an ice-cream at Giapo
4. Day trip to Rotoroa Island
5. Try stand up paddle boarding
6. Chef's Table Degustation
7. Try a glass of proper champagne
8. Fly to Queenstown for a burger
9. Try a rosé wine ice block
10. See Madonna in concert
11. Spend a weekend at Mangawhai
12. Try curling
13. Attend Auckland Writers Festival
14. Learn to juggle (still practicing)
15. Go on a wellness retreat
16. Try a powerhoop class
17. Own a Kindle Paperwhite

18. Create a print version of my eBook
19. Dye my hair a strange color – probably blue
20. Tony Robbins Seminar in Sydney
21. Girls weekend away
22. Wellington Writers Walk
23. World of Wearable Arts
24. Walk the Coast to Coast walkway from Auckland to Manukau
25. Fly in a seaplane
26. Get a blow wave at Dry and Tea
27. Liquid lunch and drunk shopping
28. Get a GHD super duper hairdryer
29. See a film in Gold Class
30. Ride on a tandem bike
31. Ride in/drive a Porsche or Aston Martin (sat in one)
32. Participate in NaNoWriMo – write a novel in a month
33. Buy an egg chair
34. Frisbee/Disc Golf
35. Ride on the back of a Harley Davidson
36. Ride in a hot air balloon
37. Publish at least one children's picture book (in progress)
38. Ride on a jet ski
39. Catch a fish (went fishing, nothing caught)
40. Tandem Skydive

APPENDIX TWO – A SELECTION OF BUCKET LIST IDEAS

Below is an assortment of four bucket list items slotted into each of the 'BUCKET' and 'TRAVEL' category templates.

The items hold no particular relevance and are in no order. They are simply meant to spark your own ideas.

Feel free to select from these lists for your own personal bucket list and organize them into categories as you see fit.

BUCKET

> B – Buy
> U – Undertakings
> C – Create
> K – Kindness
> E – Experiences
> T – Travel

Buy

- Vintage car

- Famous artwork
- Smart speaker (e.g.: Amazon Echo)
- Fitness and sleep tracker (e.g.: Fitbit)

Undertakings

- Break a world record
- Get a hole in one
- Finish a triathlon
- Master a magic trick

Create

- Knit a scarf
- Write a song
- Create a secret recipe
- Make and bury a time capsule

Kindness

- Give blood
- Visit your sponsor child
- Clean all the litter off one beach
- Volunteer in a homeless shelter for a day

Experiences

- Sumo suit wrestling
- Yoga retreat
- Get a tattoo
- Ride on a mechanical bull

TRAVEL

T – Transport
R – Restaurants and Food
A – Activities and Adventure
V – Visit
E – Experiences and Events
L – Lodging

Transport

- Ride in a sidecar of a motorcycle (Shanghai)
- Drive Route 66 (USA)
- Dogsledding (Alaska)
- Travel on the Orient Express (Europe)

Restaurants and Food

- Waste free restaurant (Melbourne)
- All glass undersea restaurant (Maldives)
- Michelin star restaurant (France)
- Try fried scorpion (Thailand)

Activities and Adventures

- Swim with whales (Tonga)
- Raft down the Grand Canyon (USA)
- Walk the Inca Trail to Machu Picchu (Peru)
- Take a trip into space

Visit

- Galapagos Islands
- Blue lagoon (Iceland)
- Game park animals (South Africa)
- Legoland (Denmark)

Experiences and Events

- Grand Prix (Monaco)
- Burning Man festival (USA)
- La Tomatina carnival (Spain)
- Northern Lights

Lodging

- Sail Hotel (Dubai)
- Overwater bungalow
- Five-star hotel or resort
- A penthouse suite

APPENDIX THREE – BUCKET LIST 100 ITEMS TEMPLATE

Feel free to use this template during the initial brainstorm of bucket list ideas or for your final list if you do not wish to organize it into categories.

MY BUCKET LIST		
1	35	69
2	36	70
3	37	71
4	38	72
5	39	73
6	40	74
7	41	75
8	42	76
9	43	77
10	44	78
11	45	79
12	46	80
13	47	81
14	48	82
15	49	83
16	50	84
17	51	85
18	52	86
19	53	87
20	54	88
21	55	89
22	56	90
23	57	91
24	58	92
25	59	93
26	60	94
27	61	95
28	62	96
29	63	97
30	64	98
31	65	99
32	66	100
33	67	
34	68	

A *NOURISH YOUR SOUL* BOOK

SUPER SEXY GOAL SETTING

THE FUN AND SIMPLE GOALS STRATEGY TO CREATE A LIFE YOU LOVE

JULIE SCHOOLER

SUPER SEXY GOAL SETTING

The Fun and Simple Goals Strategy to Create a Life You Love

-A *Nourish Your Soul* Book-

Julie Schooler

CONTENTS

1. What Are You Waiting For?   105
2. Is Super Sexy Goal Setting For You?   111
3. Goal Setting Objections   119
4. The F Word   129
5. Why Super Sexy Goal Setting Works   137
6. Five Benefits Of Super Sexy Goal Setting   143
7. Write Your Goals Wish List   149
8. Write Your Four Super Sexy Goals   157
9. Take Action (Eat Elephants And Frogs)   165
10. Goal Setting Problems And Solutions   175
11. Supercharge Your Super Sexy Goals   183
12. The Real Goal Of This Book   195

1

WHAT ARE YOU WAITING FOR?

 'Life is what happens to you when you are busy making other plans.' – John Lennon

Is This You?

- Have your previous attempts at setting goals been too difficult or overwhelming?
- Are you sick of failed goals and New Year's resolutions that go nowhere?
- Does the thought of goal setting seem so serious and boring it puts you off even attempting it?

We are promised that goal setting is an amazing way to transform our lives for the better, but it just seems like a hard chore that can often end in spectacular failure.

You may have given up on setting goals because it is frustrating and you haven't seen the results you want. Or perhaps you have never tried to set goals because the whole thing seems to take way too long and may not work, anyway.

Maybe you have spent too long working on other people's agendas and spending time and energy doing what you don't want, it is hard to even imagine focusing on what you do want and taking steps to achieve it.

But deep down you know that there is a power to setting goals. On the rare occasions you have stuck to a goal, you have felt a degree of success. You just want to find a way to set goals that excites you, a way that keeps you taking action and that enhances your life without adding to your never-ending to-do list. However, you are so busy you don't even know where to start.

You want to set goals that you KNOW will work and that will also not suck the last tiny bit of spare time and enjoyment out of your life.

Bringing Sexy Back

This book will provide you with the simplest and most fun way to set goals that will radically overhaul your life in just one year. Instead of adding to your workload, narrowing the focus to just FOUR 'super sexy' goals will remove inessential busyness and return your daily life to focusing on what is vitally important to you.

As one of the goals will focus on having fun in any way you want to think about it—relaxing on the beach with a loved one, doing a backyard waterslide with the kids or checking off some places on your travel bucket list—you will always have an element of fun as part of your four super sexy goals.

This easy-to-read guide will also cut through the confusion around how to set goals that are simple to remember and perfect for you, provide compelling reasons why super sexy goals are an essential part of life and tell you exactly what to do to work them out—even if you have never set goals before.

In less than a couple of hours this book will give you the exact blueprint to writing your own super sexy goals that span the next 12 months. You won't need to spend hours searching for information all over the Internet. You will have a clear direction and won't be confused by conflicting advice. Your new, super sexy list of only FOUR goals will help you spring out of bed every morning with renewed enthusiasm for living, not just existing.

For the first time ever, you will achieve your New Year's resolutions.

If It Works for Me...

I have set goals every year for over ten years and can see the immense power in them—if they are written and acted upon in the right way. Purely through goal setting I have achieved things I never thought possible, like running a half-marathon (even though I hated running), completing 40 bucket list items in one year and writing five books.

People ask me all the time how I am able to achieve so much. The formula is simple but extremely powerful: I set a handful of exciting, emotionally charged and meaningful goals for the year ahead. These are the super sexy goals that I want more than anything else in the next 12 months. Then I create absolute conviction around the fact that I will achieve them. I make sure I have the resources to tackle any obstacles that arise and the right mindset to face my fears. Finally, I make sure my life is ordered so I can schedule the goal tasks in and give them the focus they deserve.

I realized that I could not find one short, clear, entertaining guide on how to set and get goals this way. So I distilled the avalanche of information, and all my learnings from years of goal setting, into simple and practical tips to help you write your super sexy goals and then take action.

You gain my best insights to overcome challenges and avoid common mistakes. This book contains all the tools, advice and inspiration you need to make this your best year ever with goals that will make your heart sing.

I have written the book that I wanted to read.

BENEFITS

Just think how great it will be when you have your own super sexy goals list. There are benefits in so many areas. You will:

- rediscover buried dreams and understand your true self better
- know exactly how to determine what you want in life, not what you don't want
- feel good about yourself for following through on goals
- learn and grow by stepping out of your comfort zone
- wake up each morning with a sense of excitement and zest for life
- lead and inspire others to live life on their terms
- feel like you are living the life you were meant to live, one with excitement, meaning and true joy

APPLAUSE

Busy people are happy to recommend this book as it contains everything they need and nothing they don't for goal setting. They are excited that there is a finally a short book that helps them to effortlessly write and take action on their most appealing goals for the year. Readers are excited that there is finally a fun and easy-to-read book that removes any stigma that goal setting is boring, difficult or overwhelming.

My Promise to You

This book will make it effortless and exciting to discover your most desirable goals. This is the most fun, stress-free and of course, SEXY book on goal setting you will ever read.

You will write your goals so clearly that you will be able to recite them in your sleep and they will get you bouncing with a joy for life you had forgotten you had.

In addition, I promise that you will have a simple yet robust action plan for completing your top four super sexy goals in the next year.

It is guaranteed that if you use this book to write your goals, you will feel better, this will be your best year ever, and you will give yourself the best gift of all—a feeling of accomplishment in achieving exactly what you want in life.

Don't Be a Statistic

If you don't set goals, someone else will do it for you. You will be adrift on the sea of someone else's plan. I know that is not really what you want, but it has seemed easier up until now.

Do not wait until another year rolls by with failed New Year's resolutions to read this book. Improve your health, relationships and work or business today. Imagine how amazing your life could look in only 12 months time when you achieve your top four super sexy goals.

We often delay really living, but why and for what?

Read this book today and bring some much-needed clarity, direction and joy back into your life.

Live Life By Design

Goal setting need not be boring, complicated or serious. Four super sexy goals. One year. Your life transformed.

This book will reignite that spark you once had. You will learn how to focus on what you really want—to live life by design, not by default.

Ultimately, this book will lead you to be more enriched, fulfilled and motivated, this year and for the rest of your life.

2

IS SUPER SEXY GOAL SETTING FOR YOU?

 'Even the strongest blizzards start with a single snowflake.' – Sara Raasch

WHAT IS GOAL SETTING?

Here are a few definitions so everyone understands the basics. Then we can move on to the sexy stuff—making your life massively better.

Goal: An outcome or result that a person has committed to achieve in a set timeframe

Goal setting: Working out a plan and action steps to attain a goal

New Year's resolution: Setting a goal (resolution) especially focused on changing or improving an aspect of your life at the start of a new year

Sexy: In this context, sexy means interesting, appealing, attractive or exciting (not the arousing or erotic definition; apologies if this disappoints you!)

Super sexy goal setting: Deciding on and writing down four super sexy goals for the next 12 months and having unwavering dedication and a surefire action plan to achieve them

Goal setting, in a traditional sense, may be thought of as hard, serious and prone to failure. Super sexy goal setting is easy, fun and guaranteed to work if you commit to it.

WHO IS THIS BOOK FOR?

This book is for anyone from 9 to 90 who wants to live a more fulfilling and fun life by setting goals and taking action to achieve them. If you can check those rather large boxes, then this book is for you.

Super sexy goal setting is NOT for you if you want your life to stay exactly the same. It is NOT for you if you wish your life to get better but you can't really commit to doing anything to change it. And it is NOT for you if you are not willing to write your goals down.

This book is especially NOT for you if you are content with being average. The average person in the Western world is broke and unhappy. Don't believe me? A survey from 2015 found that over 40% of US households had less than $2,000 in savings. Over a third of Americans have saved absolutely nothing for retirement. Over 300 million people globally suffer from depression—and that is just the reported statistics! Despite anti-depression drugs not working in a third of cases, anti-depressant use has increased over 60% in the past decade. The World Health Organization has singled out depression as the leading cause of disability globally, beating out cancer and heart disease combined.

Oh, and this book is NOT for you if you don't like straight up talk and hard truths.

Super sexy goal setting is the most fun you will ever have setting goals, but there is still work to do. You must be prepared to figure out and write down four goals. And you need to have the commitment to take some action to achieve them or at least make inroads on them in the next 12 months. Note that this can be any 12-month period and you do not have to wait for the start of a new year.

Do not worry if you have no idea what you really want and cannot even imagine how to take action in your already cluttered schedule. As long as you have a desire to change or improve your life and to give goal setting a good try, this book will take care of the rest.

It is also advantageous if you keep an open mind about new concepts and trying things out. This means that sometimes you will fail at things, and sometimes things won't happen as you would like, and you will have to learn to deal with that. Why not test whether affirmations help you with your goals or practice politely saying 'No' so you can focus on what is really important? If an idea in this book resonates, then try it, but if it doesn't, then try something else. There is a truckload of helpful tips in here— pick your favorites and see what works for your situation.

WHY I WROTE THIS BOOK

Less than 10% of people set written, positive goals each year.

Less than 10%!

I wrote this book to inspire more people to write goals. My ultimate vision is a world in which 100% of us embrace goal setting, make positive changes in our lives and experience first hand the power that goals can have in creating a fulfilling life.

Imagine the kind of world we would live in if we even doubled or tripled the current number of people who have goals. I would take an educated guess that the levels of broke and unhappy people would decrease significantly. The world would be a very different place.

This book is here to help you focus on what you really want. The average person is thinking about what they don't want. More on why this is soon. If you get nothing else out of this book except for a mindset shift that leans more towards what you want out of your life than what you don't want, then writing this book has been worth it.

People have all sorts of excuses about why they don't set goals, but if one of those reasons is that goal setting seems extraordinarily boring, then you have come to the right place. Believe me, I have read many goal setting books that are so dull and serious they almost turned me off goal setting. Me! The person who wants the entire population of the globe to adopt a goal-setting revolution!

The last reason I wrote this book is to bring a whole gigantic bouncy castle of FUN back into goal setting. We all need fun in our lives but tend to dismiss it as childish or selfish. It is neither. Instead of childish, fun is a vital element to achievement—it is much easier to achieve things with a sprinkle of joy added in. And it is definitely not selfish. If we invite grace and light into our lives, people around us will, too.

I wrote this book to inspire more people to rediscover their true desires, set goals and add a bit of fun back into their lives. Doesn't that sound sexy?

THE HALF MARATHON

The power of goal setting is best illustrated in a story from my own life.

A few years ago, I attended a motivational seminar that included a 'fire walking experience'. I had no intention of doing the fire walk, but the rest of the seminar sounded interesting so I signed up. I did end up doing the fire walk and it didn't hurt a bit. Don't ask me to explain why. All I can tell you is the feeling I got afterwards. I felt incredible. Here was something I never imagined I could do, and I did it. I walked on fire! I was invincible! I could do anything! (Big disclaimer—please do not attempt a fire walk without the proper guidance and professional oversight.)

Right after the fire walk I decided to run the Auckland half marathon, a distance of 21km or 13 miles. I had not run since I was a kid over 20 years back, and never at that distance. I had decided when I was young that I hated running and I believed it would damage my feet. So this goal was a definite challenge for me! And it didn't stop there—I had a number of obstacles to face.

The first obstacle I came up against was money. I bought the half marathon ticket. I bought new running shoes. I bought a few pairs of specially designed running socks at $30 each—$30 just for one pair of socks! I went to a podiatrist and got his opinion and bought orthotics for my new gym shoes. I ended up spending $700 before I took a single running step.

And that wasn't even the hard work—then I started running! The Auckland half marathon is something special as it gives you the chance to go on foot over the Harbor Bridge, which is vehicle only. That bridge is steep! I heard that if you didn't make it over the Harbor Bridge in a set time period a bus picked you up—and this "bus of shame" story kept me motivated to run up a lot of hills.

If someone had told me about all the things I would have to do and what I would go through before I crossed that finish line, I would have given up. But I had an absolute determination about completing the half marathon. I just knocked each obstacle out of the way—money, training, pain—it didn't matter.

One of the reasons I had such determination is that I painted a picture describing exactly what I would be doing when I achieved my goal. In this case:

> 'I have just completed the Auckland half marathon in less than 2 ½ hours and I am feeling great and my support team is patting me on the back and telling me well done'.

Completing the half marathon and doing it within 2 ½ hours—I could do that. But the really funny thing is, I was reading my goal every day before the run and I hadn't actually done anything about the support crew. As the half marathon started very early in the morning I had organized for my boyfriend to drop me at the start line and then I was to call him when I got to the end to pick me up. I was running by myself and no one was going to meet me at the finish line.

Well, as I turned the corner and ran the last part towards the finish line, I heard my name being called—"Julie, Julie". I looked over to where all the people were crowded watching the runners and there was my Dad and my sister, Natalie, and a couple of friends, all waving and cheering me on.

I got to the finish line and they all came and found me straight away, giving me hugs, patting my back, shaking my hand and telling me well done.

In short, even though I didn't plan or force it that way, my goal happened EXACTLY how I wrote it down.

BE EXCEPTIONAL

I want more people to experience the pure magic of the decisive focus, conviction and vividly described goals that form super sexy goal setting. You will feel a major sense of achievement in setting and achieving four goals in one year. And you will grow as a person as you step out of your comfort zone and create memories out of your dreams. I don't want you to be average. I want you to be exceptional.

> This is a short book but—and this is not said lightly—it
> WILL change your life.

If you are a 'get to the point' person, then feel free to skip the next few chapters and go straight to Chapter Seven. From that point on are all the strategies you need to decide on your four super sexy goals and start taking action on them. However, mindset is a major part of the success of goal setting, so if you need a bit more convincing that this is for you, keep reading right through.

3

GOAL SETTING OBJECTIONS

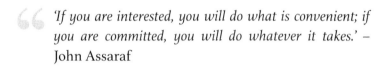 *'If you are interested, you will do what is convenient; if you are committed, you will do whatever it takes.'* – John Assaraf

REASONS VERSUS EXCUSES

So why do you not have goals right now, or why are you not following through on goals you have made? There are plenty of seemingly valid reasons not to have goals or to let them fall away into oblivion.

It is important to review the main goal-setting objections well, objectively. The next chapter will dive into the underlying reasons why we voice these excuses in the first place (hint: it is a four-letter word starting with F). For now, let's bust apart these stories.

'GOAL SETTING SEEMS WAY TOO COMPLICATED'

Goal setting looks like a lot of hard work, you don't know where to start and it may not even work, so why bother? On the surface, this really does look like a valid reason. Just a quick delve into goals and goal-setting literature brings up more questions than answers. For example:

- Don't I have to have a life plan in place and know my purpose before writing my goals?
- Should I write small, achievable goals to make me feel like a success or big, hairy audacious goals ('BHAGs') to stretch myself?
- Are goals the same as desires, dreams, wishes or wants?
- Do I focus on the end goal or what I will learn along the way?
- How are habits, routines, systems and resolutions tied in with goals?
- What areas of my life should I cover when setting goals?
- How many goals should I write in total and for each area of my life?
- Should I be writing goals out for the next week, month, year, five years, ten years, the whole rest of my life?
- Is it a good idea to map out all action steps and have a plan with the goal?

No wonder less than 10% of the population writes goals. With that list of bewilderment and confusion, I am surprised even small percentages embark on goal setting.

Forget about the answers to the questions above. With super sexy goal setting, you will be focusing on four challenging yet achievable goals for one year. You will be shown the very best way to write them so you are excited about them. You will get tips on how to put them into action and keep the momentum going.

Super sexy goals strip away the extra stuff and only focus on what is most important and what works.

'I AM WAY TOO BUSY AND DON'T HAVE TIME FOR GOALS'

Having goals may seem like a good idea, but on top of a busy life, adding goals to the mix seems like an impossible ask. You may have work, kids, a partner, a household to run. You have a big full life. If you can't spend three minutes in the bathroom in peace, writing out goals and taking action on them is just crazy talk.

Being busy is a competitive sport these days, and everyone looks like they are striving for the gold medal for 'busy champion of the world'. Are you really so busy you cannot spend some time on what is most important to you? Many people mistake movement for achievement. Everyone has the same number of hours in the day, but the successful few prioritize what is really essential and delegate or eliminate the rest.

The truth is that selecting well-written and clear goals will actually cut the busyness and overwhelm out of your life. You NEED goals to gain clarity and rid yourself of the busy parts that add nothing to your life. Right now, you may not think anything can be removed from your life to make way for goals, but if you find the right goals to focus and work on, other parts of your life will shift to accommodate what is truly important to you.

You will write four goals. These are the four most crucial things to focus on for the next 12 months. If something comes up, ask yourself, "Is this thing more important than my top four goals?"

> The vital part to remember is that goals will reduce, not increase, what you really need to do.

Be honest with yourself and don't say you don't have time. Admit that you don't have priorities. Acknowledge that you don't have clarity. Concede that not making decisions about what is really important is a way to absolve yourself from determining your destiny.

'Don't I have to know my life's purpose first?'

If you do have a purpose already, great, but it is NOT a prerequisite for choosing goals. You don't need to work out your whole life plan or your vision or mission statement or what you want your legacy to be. Phew! What a relief that all that serious navel gazing work can be jettisoned.

To flip this thought around, goal setting can help determine a more purposeful direction in life. You often don't know what your passions are until you work on them. The occasional few laps in the pool and bike to work becomes triathlon training. Writing in your journal each morning starts your memoir. Salsa dancing lessons with your partner take you to a regional competition.

At the very least, taking action on your goals helps you acquire skills that may come in handy later when you have figured it all out. Steve Jobs took a calligraphy class at college that later in his life had a major influence on the design of Apple products. He could never have known that taking one random college class would have had an impact on the typography of personal computers all over the world.

'I set goals in the past and it didn't work out'

Do you give up on other things in your life or decide not to commit anymore, as you 'know' it won't work? How is that working out for you?

Failure is a big reason why people do not set goals, and this will be explored more in the next chapter. The main question to answer here is WHY you failed at your goals. There are so many reasons for a goals failure that you can't just dismiss all goals for the rest of time as 'bad'. Instead, delve into why the goal didn't work so you can rectify a specific weak spot.

Perhaps the goals were not written properly, or at all, usually in the case of New Year's resolutions. Maybe they were not exciting or compelling enough to keep your interest up. Perhaps there wasn't enough structure in place—scheduling or deadlines—to carry on with them. Maybe you wrote too many or they were in conflict. Competing goals will be explored in Chapter Ten—this can be a major reason why goals don't work. Examining exactly why your goals failed can tell you what to do differently next time.

And there will be a next time. With these four super sexy goals, there will be minimal chance that you will lose interest, won't schedule them in or have a conflict so you will be more likely to continue with your goals.

'I am worried about what others might think'

If you set goals and publicly announce them, then you have some accountability, which is a good way to stay on track. However, this can have the reverse effect: if for some reason you don't achieve your goal or it is a goal that people don't like, then you face public scrutiny.

First, you don't have to tell everyone about your goals. If you really think it is a good way to stay accountable and the downside of possible negative judgment doesn't bother you, then by all means splash your goals all over social media. But if you think that it will actually decrease your motivation, then keep your goals to yourself or only tell a couple of close friends who will be cheerleaders for you no matter what.

Second, who cares what people think? Unless they are paying your electricity bill, they have no say in your life. Remember most people don't set goals and most people end up broke and unhappy, so do you really want to take on opinions from the average person?

And last, most people don't care or notice, anyway. They are not judging you. They are competing for 'busy champion of the world' or staring at their phones. People only really care if it affects them, and what you are doing probably doesn't.

'I AM NOT THE GOAL SETTING TYPE'

You have decided you are not the type of person who has goals. Goal setting doesn't suit your personality or the way you live your life. Deciding that 'I am' something that is contradictory to being a goal setter is a great story to tell yourself to get out of it. It is so believable as you have tied your identity to not liking goal setting. Once you put 'I am' in front of something, it seems like a fixed truth even though it is simply a limiting belief.

You may say positive things about yourself that imply having goals is bad. For instance, 'I am spontaneous' or 'I am fun loving' or 'I live in the present and am not ambitious'. But people who set goals don't think of themselves as rigid, dull or ruthless. Instead they think goals give them more chance of an exciting life, of reaching their potential and adding value into the world. How you frame yourself against your belief about goals makes a big difference.

Strangely, you can even paint yourself in a negative light to get out of writing goals. 'I am a procrastinator' is a primary example.

You are not a procrastinator! You may sometimes procrastinate if you don't like what you are doing or are feeling tired or are scared of the next step, but it is an outside factor. It is not you. If someone put a gun to your head and said you had to get X done, you wouldn't tell them 'But I am a procrastinator'. You would do it. Immediately.

'MY LIFE IS PRETTY GOOD SO WHY STRIVE FOR MORE?'

This little gem of an untruthful 'truth' crops up in different ways. In the excuses that 'My kids need me' or 'I will wait until the kids are older'. Or perhaps a guilt trip notion of 'I have enough already' or 'Who am I to ask for more when I have so much?'

Your kids need role models to show them that goals can be set and achieved. They need to see someone striving to be their very best. They need to be shown first hand how to fail well—pick themselves up, dust themselves off and keep going. They NEED you to set goals.

You owe it to the world to use up every single tiny ounce of all the resources and riches that you were so fortunately bestowed with to reach your potential, create value and share your gifts with the world. It would be a travesty if you just settled because you thought you didn't deserve even more from life.

And are you really happy in every area of your life? Probably not. We tell ourselves we love our comfort zones because outside of them is a scary place. More on comfort zones in the next chapter. But for now, be honest with yourself. Are you dissatisfied in some areas of your life? Good! Get excited, as now you may be willing to take action.

'I AM TOO...'

There are tons of other reasons why people decide to not set goals, and this would be a very long chapter if I itemized each one.

Too tired? Goals actually give you a renewed sense of purpose that helps you spring out of bed in the morning. Not only will prioritizing what you want and focusing on the most important goals give you clarity but also more energy.

Too expensive? Well some can be. Space shuttle flights are still a tad pricey. So choose goals that don't cost a lot or that can actually save you money. Learning to cook a great meal, writing a book or going for a swim all cost pennies and actually help you become healthier and happier.

You are not too old. You are not too young. You are not too uneducated or too poor, and you are not too busy. You are not too purple or too green or any other 'too' you tell yourself you are. You are not too late. Too late only applies when the zombie apocalypse happens, not before.

The last chapter gave you a taster of how frank I can be, but think of this book as more of an honest coach to you than a sympathetic friend. Your objections to goals and goal setting are just excuses so you can feel okay about your average life. They help you justify why you are not trying to reach your full potential. They are stories you tell to yourself that make it tolerable that you are not taking action on your dreams. They help you feel good about settling for mediocrity.

CHOOSE YOUR HARD

Overall, many of the objections we have stem from an inherent conflict where we want to be content with our present lives while also wanting a better future. For instance, we want to treat our bodies with respect and kindness but also acknowledge we want to tone up and lose a little weight. It is hard to juggle this paradox. But just because it is hard doesn't meant that goal setting is wrong. It is natural to want more.

> The key to a successful life is to appreciate where we currently are but still constantly improve, dream and plan.

This will be said a few times throughout the book: getting your head around this present versus future conflict is hard. Not doing anything with your life because you are using a silly paradox or some other thing as an excuse is also hard. Choose your hard.

These objections all have the same underlying cause. Let us delve into the real reason for all this anti-goal-setting sentiment in the next chapter.

4

THE F WORD

 'Avoiding danger is no safer in the long run than outright exposure. The fearful are caught as often as the bold.' – Helen Keller

The Real Reason

We were able to smash though all those seemingly valid reasons to avoid goal setting in the previous chapter with a bit of logic and common sense, so why do we offer up so many objections against goals? There has to be something underlying the myriad excuses.

That something is, of course... drum roll please... dah, dah, de, dah... FEAR. We don't set goals, we give up on goals and we don't take action on goals because we are afraid.

There are a number of reasons why we are scared of setting goals, including being worried about rejection, disapproval, making the wrong decision or missing out on something else. Even success and accomplishment can make people scared. If you stand out, you can be knocked down. Or you don't want to start something in case you achieve a goal and it does not make you as happy or successful as you expected.

The biggest fear for the vast majority is a fear of failure. Let us take a closer look at failure and hopefully get a new perspective on it.

FAILURE

Understandably, goal setting is associated with a fear of failure. You may set a goal that does not work out. This can mean a loss of time that could have been spent on something else, a loss of money, even a loss of something bigger—a house, a business, friends, your reputation in the community. Of course you fear failure if you associate it with loss in this way, but there are ways to look at failure that don't have such serious implications.

First, be sensible with your goal setting by making sure you don't set goals that have more than a tiny chance of catastrophic loss. If you want to start a new business, don't quit your job and mortgage your house up to the hilt. Start slowly, on the side. Dream big and also plan your goals to minimize the downside.

Second, know that you will fail. Oh you will fail. Sometimes you will fall down so spectacularly and so hard that you are not sure if your tailbone will ever feel right again. But you will also learn to get back up, dust yourself off and keep going. Whether that means overcoming an obstacle to get to the goal, or making a decision to veer onto another goal, your true character is built not on whether you fail but on how and when you pick yourself back up again. Maybe next time you will fail better! Failure is part of goal setting—you need to find a way to be okay with that.

Third, the thought of failure shouldn't stop you from trying. Perhaps you only write half a book by the deadline, or only make a few dollars in your side business or cross the finish line after everyone else has gone home. So what? You did better than everyone who never tried. You can do it again and do it better. You learned a lot, gained skills, and now you know what to focus on to improve next time.

> If you shoot for the stars and only land on the moon, you can still be proud of what you achieved.

Last, know that all the most successful people have failed. Failed big time. Failure means that you are playing this game called life, not sitting on the sidelines. This list may help you feel better about any failures that happen to you in your goal-setting journey:

- Oprah Winfrey was fired from her first TV job at a local news station as she was 'unfit for television'.
- J.K. Rowling's *Harry Potter* manuscript was rejected by all 12 major publishers.
- Elvis Presley failed an audition to become part of a vocalist quartet as he was told he 'couldn't sing'.
- Walt Disney was fired from his newspaper job because he 'lacked imagination and had no good ideas'.
- George Lucas' script for *Star Wars* was turned down by two major film studios, and 20th Century Fox only took it on because of his exemplary reputation even though they didn't understand it.
- Michael Jordan, at 15, was passed up for his high school basketball team.

Jordan is credited with saying that, "I've missed more than 9,000 shots in my career. I've lost almost 300 games. And 26 times, I've been trusted to take the game winning shot and missed. I've failed over and over and over again in my life. And that is why I succeed."

Three Levels of Fear

Susan Jeffers says in her classic personal development book, *Feel the Fear and do it Anyway*, that fear has three levels:

1. Surface story: These are the excuses and objections we discussed in the previous chapter—the 'I am too busy / tired / old' story.
2. Inner states of mind: This is the fear of failure, success, rejection, disapproval or missing out, etc., described above.
3. I Can't Handle It!: At the bottom of every one of your fears is simply the fear that you cannot handle whatever life may bring you.

The real reason you do not set goals is because you do not think you can handle what life brings you as a result of setting the goal. This may be the thought that you won't be able to tackle the obstacles that arise, or you won't be able to deal with the outcome of the goal itself. Why do you think, 'I Can't Handle It'? Where does this underlying fear come from?

It comes from The Lizard.

The Lizard

Not a pet lizard, but The Lizard that resides in your brain. You are evolutionarily hardwired for survival. In prehistoric times, humans needed a robust flight-or-fight-or-freeze mechanism for when we spotted a sabre tooth tiger, or when it spotted us. In your head right this very moment is a little area near the brain stem called the amygdala, and it prompts you to constantly scan for anything that can kill you.

As this is a survival tool from a primitive era, the author, coach, and wise soul, Martha Beck, describes this part of you as 'The Lizard'. The Lizard is a reptilian animal in your brain that perks its head up and alerts you to anything you perceive as scary or scarce. It does this to protect you, but it means your brain is wired to find the negative at all times.

The Lizard tells you things are scary even if they are not. It alters your perception. In the Western world, you live in one of the most abundant and safe times in human history. As there is nothing really dangerous going on, The Lizard turns its attention to other things it thinks you might like to worry about.

Your Lizard now tells you day in and day out that you lack time, energy, money or love. Think about that for a moment: instead of being scarce in water, food or shelter, your Lizard brain is trying to protect you by telling you that time, energy, money or love are scarce and need to be conserved. It is fake fear, but it feels very real.

Due to your Lizard fear you now don't want to do anything to jeopardize all the existing time, energy, money or love you currently have. Even if you are dissatisfied with your life, your Lizard tells you not to try and strive for more in case you lose it all. Because if you lose it all, it says you can't handle it.

THE COMFORT ZONE

What your Lizard and its accompanying fear of 'I can't handle it' do is keep you in your comfort zone. People think they don't want to leave their comfort zones, as it feels pleasant and familiar, and they feel safe and in control of their environments. Going to work, coming back to your home, watching TV, these are all nice at times. Being in your comfort zone is comfortable, but after a while it actually starts to hurt you. You start to feel unenthused and jaded with your routine existence.

Stepping out of your comfort zone and trying new things leads to growth, and growth is necessary for a fulfilling life. Successful people are prepared to step outside their comfort zones. The real magic happens there, so even if it feels uneasy at first, you must try to counter the Lizard and your fears and go for your goals.

Most people do not realize they live pretty crappy lives by not really trying to accomplish what they can and to realize their potential.

DANCE WITH THE FEAR

Your Lizard and its 'I can't handle it' fear signal has been a driving force that has kept you in your comfort zone. Then your mind has made up stories to make you feel better about playing small in the one life you are gifted with.

But please, please, please don't beat yourself up about this. Do something with this newfound wisdom instead.

The paradoxical truth about fear is that it will never go away unless you go out and do the thing you fear. The only way to blast away the fear is to take action. Set goals, learn, grow. Don't fight the fear or hide from it, dance with fear instead.

The past two chapters have conquered your objections to goal setting and explained that the best way to overcome your fears is to take action on your goals. The next two chapters will explain what the super sexy goal system is, why it will work for you and all its super sexy benefits.

5

WHY SUPER SEXY GOAL SETTING WORKS

 'Motivation is what gets you started. Habit is what keeps you going.'– Jim Rohn

SUPER SEXY GOAL SETTING OVERVIEW

Super sexy goal setting is deciding on and writing down four super sexy goals for the next 12 months and having unwavering dedication and a surefire action plan to achieve them.

WHY 12 MONTHS?

Choosing goals that take a year allows a clear deadline to be in place but also provides enough time to complete something challenging. Both these factors make you feel like you have accomplished something worthwhile.

This can be any 12-month period. You don't have to start at the beginning of the calendar year. Start now! Also, you can do all four goals over the entire 12-month period or focus on particular goals in certain periods within the year, say one each quarter. Think ONE YEAR. No more than that.

Why four goals?

You will get more done by doing less. Focusing on four goals keeps your finite amounts of attention, time and resources narrowed on the most important areas of your life that you want to improve. There are a lot of good things to do, but narrowing down to four makes you focus only on the great things. As author Jim Collins argues: "good is the enemy of the great". Remember you only have 12 months. You can do another four next year! Think FOUR GOALS. No more than that.

What areas should the goals cover?

You can choose any area of your life in which to set goals. Start with the part of your life with which you are most dissatisfied. If you want to follow the exact system in this book, then choose one goal for each of the three main areas of your life—health, relationships and work/business. The fourth area is called 'just for you'—something fun or a hobby or a skill to master or an exciting challenge. Think FOUR AREAS. No more than that.

Why It Works

The reason super sexy goal setting is different from other goal-setting strategies is that it makes goals exciting, easy to action and emotionally fulfilling. It compels you to actually want to set goals and achieve them.

It does this by weaving some of the core principles from psychology and personal development into its system. These then allow you to rediscover your power to create the life you truly desire. Let's take a brief look at these concepts.

PAIN AND PLEASURE

No matter what stories you tell yourself, the only reason you don't have goals is that you have linked more pain or less pleasure to having the goal than to not having it. Your equation up until now is goal equals pain or no goal equals pleasure.

Pain and pleasure are the major drivers of animal behavior. Everything we do in life is driven by our need to avoid pain or gain pleasure. We think we are complex beings, humans with imagination and emotion and conscious decision-making abilities, but when it comes down to it we are just like Pavlov's dogs.

Think about it: why did that New Year's Resolution to go for a run every morning fail? Because getting out of your cozy bed in the dark and cold seems more painful than hitting the snooze button. Why did you give up on writing that book? Because the latest binge-watching sensation seemed much more enjoyable than wrestling with words on a blank document.

The key to an outstanding life is utilizing these unavoidable drivers to our advantage. Link extraordinary amounts of pleasure to taking action on goals and not attempting a goal to massive, immediate pain. Switch around the equation. Goal equals pleasure. No goal equals pain.

The way the super sexy goal system works is to link huge amounts of pleasure to your goals. There are only four goals, there is a relatively short time frame, they are written in the most desirable way and one of the goals is an exciting or fun challenge just for you, so there is a lot of enjoyment woven in. Not getting the goal automatically starts to feel immensely painful.

Willpower and Momentum

People think they need a whole truckload of willpower to accomplish goals. Thank goodness that this is incorrect as willpower is a fickle beast. It gets used up especially fast on those crazy days when your youngest vomits all over the carpet and you have a flat tire.

You only need a pinch of willpower to start creating some momentum. Once you have momentum there is no stopping you. You need to nudge the boulder off its ledge, and then it will start to tumble down the hill on its own. So how do you kick start willpower? There are only two ways to start to do something. Either you are pushed into it or pulled into it.

If you are pushed you are told to do it, or you are paid to do it, or you are cajoled somehow, say with bribes or rewards. No one likes this sleazy salesman approach much, but with goals, 'push motivation' is helpful to get you through a hard patch. Can't seem to start a new exercise routine? Booking a non-refundable personal training session will get you to the gym. Don't want to finish writing that next chapter? A reward of chocolate or TV could help.

Ultimately what you want is an abundance of 'pull motivation'. You want to want it. You don't want to reluctantly fork out money to the sleazy salesman. You want to happily hand over your credit card. With goals, pull motivation means you go to the gym and work out hard because you enjoy the strength and energy you gain from it. It means you write the next chapter because you are excited to see the characters come alive on the page or you can't wait to share the story with the world. Look, this won't happen all the time with all your goals, but when it does it is magical. Knowing it can happen is a good start.

Super sexy goal setting takes into account both push and pull motivations to create momentum, rather than relying on willpower. Push motivations such as deadlines, accountability and rewards are all optional parts of the system. In addition, pull motivation is linked to every aspect of the goals strategy. It is included in the positive way they are written right through to tools to help you feel great on the journey to achieving your goals.

What Successful People Do

The real reason goals fail is that you don't take enough account of underlying beliefs and emotions. You only do something because of how you think it will make you feel. The average person feels fearful of goals and associates them with pain. The successful person dances with the fear and links goals to pleasure, no matter what.

Turning tasks that are good for you but you initially dislike into pleasurable experiences is the secret to a meaningful and fulfilling life. The most successful people do the things that the average person won't do. They make a habit of being uncomfortable.

For goals this means you must find a way to change your belief to add joy to something that might not initially be thought of as easy or fun. Whether you use rewards or find ways to inherently love the journey, you must make the next action taken on a goal as enjoyable as possible.

The key to successfully completing goals is converting

tasks that you may not like but are good for you into
positive experiences that you want to do.

The good news is that this principle is woven into the fabric of
the super sexy goal system. You don't have to worry about how
you will dramatically transform your beliefs overnight. Just
follow the system and they will naturally be revolutionized.

This chapter told you exactly what the super sexy goal-setting
system is and gave you a peek behind the curtain of why it is so
powerful. Let us look at some benefits of super sexy goals to
finish off this mindset part of the book so we can get you juiced
up to take action on writing your goals.

6
_____

FIVE BENEFITS OF SUPER SEXY GOAL SETTING

 'It's about being alive and feisty and not sitting down and shutting up even though people would like you to.' – P!nk, singer

1. A Little Bit Naughty

You can't have *Super Sexy Goal Setting* as a title of a book without the whole thing feeling a little bit naughty. I want you to dismiss the notion that goals are for boring, organized, responsible people. I want you to take that idea out of your head.

Finding goals that challenge you as a person, that help you grow and allow you to focus on what is really important, is an ultimate rebellion against the system.

Goal setting is an act of defiance to a culture that wants you to be continuously distracted, overwhelmed with day-to-day priorities and focused on the next material purchase to make you feel good.

Super sexy goal setting is a way to make you feel more alive and in control of the one life you have.

Be a rebel. Set some goals.

Here are four other benefits of super sexy goal setting.

2. You Don't Have to Know Your Purpose

You don't need to work out your purpose in life to decide on four goals for the next 12 months. If you do already know it, great, use it to give you some direction in choosing your goals. But it is not a mandatory part of the goal-setting process.

If you decide that you need to know your purpose before you embark on goals, then you make goal setting needlessly complicated, it takes a lot more time, and in the way of all good procrastination attempts, it may stop you from setting any goals at all.

Of course finding your purpose in life is so important that I will be writing a book on it, but for the moment, let us jump in the deep end. Set some goals, achieve some goals, see that the process works, get momentum and take action on more goals. This is more important than navel gazing right now.

The really great thing about choosing four goals and having a short time span in which to achieve them is that taking action on the goals makes you much more likely to work out direction and meaning for your life. Instead of thinking purpose comes before action, action can actually precede purpose. How can you know your entire life's purpose until you try something and see if you can stick to it for 12 months?

Linking everything to a life's purpose sounds so heavy. Instead, with super sexy goal setting you take a lighter approach: pick a direction, start down that path and see if you like it. If you like it, continue: create a positive habit, master a skill, grow as a person. And if you don't, you have gained valuable feedback about what your life's purpose is not going to be about.

3. Incorporating Goals Leads to LESS Overwhelm

You would think that if you add four goals into an already hectic life, you are going to stress yourself out. But the opposite is true.

These goals help you focus on what is really important in your life. As they are the most important things, other things have to take a back seat or be eliminated altogether. Yes, you still have to pick your kids up from school, do your tax returns and floss, but a lot of the superfluous extra busyness will fall way when you build up your prioritizing muscle. You won't feel the need to mindlessly swipe a screen or get caught up in the next binge watch sensation —you have more important things to do.

The fact that you are taking on no more than four goals for one year means you can be concrete about exactly what you need to get done. You are not thinking abstractly way into the future. In addition, this book gives you tools, such as how to reduce decision making in other areas of your life and how to say 'No' politely so you have more time for your goals.

4. It is KISS not SMART

The whole super sexy goal setting system is set up to be as simple as possible because if it is not simple it doesn't get done. Four goals. One year. Written in a way that inspires action and commitment. Achieve more by doing less. That is it.

Goal setting advice makes things needlessly complicated by saying goals should adhere to the 'SMART' acronym. This is my little rant about why SMART is for dummies.

SMART is an acronym that stands for Specific, Measurable, Action, Realistic and Time. Except it doesn't! Sometimes the acronym has Achievable for the A and Relevant for the R. Plus, Time seems to be time-bound, timeframe, time or changed to temporal on occasion. No one agrees on what SMART even stands for, so why are we trying to use that acronym to set our goals?

Moreover, it gives five criteria for setting goals in a kind of abstract way. You have to go back and forth between the specific goal you are trying to write and whether it checks off against each of the criteria (which can't be agreed upon, anyway). By the time you make sure your goal is SMART, you have done so much work you feel like you have achieved your goal when all you have done is achieved the almost impossible task of writing it down 'correctly'.

Lastly, writing a SMART goal, if you are even able to do it, leads to a goal that doesn't have an emotional connection, a vivid portrait of how you will feel and what you will be doing when you get your goal. It is not compelling enough to drive you to take action.

I have an acronym to replace SMART: KISS—keep it simple, stupid.

5. A Major Focus on Fun

What sets super sexy goal setting apart from the rest is its focus on fun. One goal is just for you. There are no rules here—it is whatever fun looks like to you. It can be exciting (e.g.: travel to exotic places), relaxing (e.g.: reading a novel) or challenging yourself to improve a skill (e.g.: learning a musical instrument).

Why fun at all? Unless we focus on fun, on something we actually enjoy, we will burn out from the other goals and all the other day-to-day activities. This is a positive experience we inherently enjoy, not one we make ourselves like.

Why a goal around fun? One reason is that most people don't emphasize fun in their lives, and it is so important that the only way you may actually do it is to set a goal around doing it. You crave the sweetness of fun at a deep level but disregard it as not important. Then that sweetness you want gets turned into food cravings and before you know it you have devoured an entire block of chocolate. Deciding on fun in a structured way should eliminate it overtaking you in less desirable ways.

The biggest benefit to this fun goal is that you can use it as a reward for completing the other goals with which you may be having a harder time. Yes, you should try and transform experiences you dislike into something more enjoyable, but sometimes things are just hard and the best way to get through them is with some push motivation—bribing or rewarding yourself. So do a hard task and then plan your next vacation or read a few chapters of a novel or strum on your guitar and get the added feeling you are working towards another goal at the same time.

It is a one-two punch of double awesomeness.

Mindset Conclusion

You are half way through the book and you haven't written down a single goal yet. I mean whaaaaat? This first part of the book has been essential to bake in more positive beliefs around goal setting.

You have now learned that no matter what sort of person you are, you can write goals and you will benefit from goal setting. All you need to create things in your life is for your desire to be greater than your fear.

By now you are starting to understand that your emotions, your beliefs and your identity are far more important than willpower, plans and habits. You don't get your goals—you get what you believe you are—your identity.

Sometimes you don't need to learn anything new to achieve real transformation, but instead to UNLEARN what you 'know' or believe. By cracking open those limiting beliefs, you start to rediscover what your heart is telling you to do. Deep down you know what you want; you just have to listen carefully to catch the whispers of your soul.

You have been promised more time, less overwhelm, more fun and less struggle with this super sexy system. If this all seems too good to be true, read on and judge for yourself. The next two chapters will guide you to four written goals that you are genuinely excited about. Let's begin.

7

WRITE YOUR GOALS WISH LIST

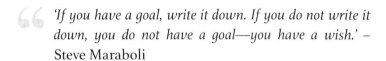

'If you have a goal, write it down. If you do not write it down, you do not have a goal—you have a wish.' – Steve Maraboli

GOALS WISH LIST

By the end of this chapter you will have a written list of what you want in life. This is not your final goals list. It is definitely not a to-do list. It is simply a 'goals wish list' to capture your dreams down on paper.

Your list MUST be written down. Writing ideas down makes them real, gets your thoughts in order and is a permanent record of your wants and dreams. Studies have shown that you boost your chances of accomplishing goals by at least 40% if they are written down. A goal that is not in writing is merely a hope or wishful thinking. Writing starts your mind conspiring how the goal could be possible. It creates momentum. Write down your goals wish list!

This may seem simple, but it can be more difficult than you originally thought due to the belief that goal setting must be hard or complicated, your innate ability to focus on what you don't want and how easily distracted humans can be.

You don't have to decide whether this is a 'worthy' goal right now. You don't need to write it in the 'best' way or figure out action steps. And you definitely don't need to think about deadlines or timelines.

Step One: Brainstorm

We are so easily distracted these days, so this will be a timed writing exercise—an hour would be great, but even 20 minutes would be a start. No phones, no Internet.

What you need: something on which to write out your goals wish list—a blank document on your computer, or a large piece of paper or the back of an envelope. Anything will do. Gather up some pens or colored markers as well, if needed. Then find something with which to time yourself—a watch, phone timer or a giant hourglass, for example. Don't do anything else in the time you set aside for this exercise.

Now brainstorm, free write or mind map EVERYTHING you have always wanted to do, see, have, be, meet, etc. You know in your heart what you want.

Have fun with this creative exercise. Be silly, invoke your curiosity, think outside the box. Think about fun things, challenging things, short-term activities, long-term pastimes, local places to visit and trips abroad. Think of your interests, hobbies, and passions. Think of different areas of your life, for instance: health, relationships, work, finances, personal growth, contribution.

Dream big. Go wild. Get ridiculous. Get unreasonable. Anything goes. Just write.

Write in short bullet points or long, descriptive paragraphs. Know that anything can be changed or deleted later. Don't worry whether you are describing outcomes or performance-based goals. Don't worry that you don't have time or can't afford it or allow in any other negative thoughts. Don't worry if it seems too exotic or difficult, or conversely, too mundane or easy. If it lights a fire in your belly, then it is perfect. Don't think it is not possible. If someone else in the world has done it, it is possible. Write down what you want in any way that makes sense to you.

Due to your Lizard brain perpetually scanning for danger, you have a bias to pick up negatives much more than positives, so you can often think about what you don't want, rather than what you do want. Use this to your advantage. If you don't like something in your life, or there is something that you can't put up with a moment longer—good! Write that down and then flip it so you can think of a solution. For example, "I don't like the extra pounds I put on" can be flipped to, "I want to lose weight or eat healthier."

If you can't flip, then write down what you don't want. For instance, I don't want to feel this tired, put up with this crappy relationship any longer or be paid so low. This can be a good way to start and will clear the way to what you DO want.

Remember at this point that this does not have to look pretty. It is just a wish list—it will be narrowed down and tidied up later. Writing goals, any goals, is the only important thing.

There is no 'right number' of entries to end on. Just write until you run out of steam or time is up. Then reset your timer and use questions and prompts below to add to and define your wants and dreams even more.

. . .

Step Two: Questions and Prompts

Questions and prompts help you to figure out more goals wish list items and also focus on finding items more attuned to you. Using questions has been found to have a massive impact, because if a question is asked, even if it is not spoken aloud, your mind is still compelled to answer it.

There are four general areas of questions. You don't have to answer all these questions. They are just there as prompts so you can add to your goals wish list or to refine it so it reflects YOU.

Santa's Knee Questions

These come in various forms, but overall they help you think like an excited five-year-old sitting on Santa's knee. There are no filters, no limits, no boundaries. Go crazy. Ask for the impossible. For example:

- What would you like if there were no financial limits?
- What would you do if you had unlimited time, money and resources?
- If you won a huge lottery, what would you do?
- If fear were not part of the equation what would you do?
- If you were given three wishes, what would you wish for (excluding world peace, of course)?

Deathbed Regrets Questions

These help you confront your own mortality. For example:

- What would you like to have said about you in your eulogy?

- What do you absolutely HAVE to do before you die?
- What would be your biggest regret on your deathbed?
- What would you do, see, or have if you only had one year to live?

Passions and Interests Questions

These help you to remember what you have always liked to do, or thought you would be good at but then decided that time, money or something else was in the way. These can be one-off things or longer-term hobbies. For example:

- What was your childhood dream to do, see, create?
- What have you always wanted to do but you felt like you didn't have time?
- What do you want to buy or do just to have fun?
- What would you do even without pay?
- What activity makes you lose track of time?
- What has always been one of your biggest dreams in life?
- What would be a perfect day for you?

Get Down to Specifics Questions

Here are some questions that can help you think about your wish list in alternative ways.

- What would you DO—see or create or accomplish?
- Where would you like to visit or travel—countries, places, locations?
- What new foods do you want to taste?
- Who do you want to meet in person?

- What experiences do you want to have?
- What activities do you want to try at least once?
- What activities or skills do you want to learn or master?
- What adventures would get you out of your comfort zone?
- Are there any special moments or scheduled events you want to witness?

STEP THREE: NARROW IT DOWN

How good was that!? How do you feel?

You have done something most people never do. The average person spends more time on working out what is for dinner than what he wants out of life.

Now I want you to pick FOUR goals that you can focus on for the next 12 months and discard the rest.

Whaaaaat!?

Don't throw them away completely—keep your wish list somewhere you can find it again. But after you have chosen your four goals, don't refer to it for 12 months.

Yikes!

This may be such a hard ask that it makes you want to stop the goal setting altogether. Please don't do that, you have come this far and now you just need to make a decision or two.

We live in a world where we can do anything, but prioritizing what is really important is an essential skill. It is easier than ever in this day and age to get ideas, but it's also easy to be overwhelmed, have your focus split and then get burned out. You need to narrow down to four super sexy goals. I know you like many of these goals, but remember good is the enemy of the great.

The first way to decide on four goals is to go through your list and find the ones that jump out at you, that your gut instinct tells you would be amazing to do, that really excite you. If you are not really excited, then why is it a goal? Circle those.

Next, get a bit practical and decide what you could actually do in the next 12 months. This should only take out the very long-term goals—perhaps building your dream home or flying to the moon —but you could create a one-year goal around getting to the larger goals. Circle the ones that fit.

Last, if you want to keep your goals balanced across your life, then find one goal in each of the main categories: health, relationships and work/business, plus one fun or challenge goal just for you. Circle the best goals out of those categories.

> In short, select four goals that are exciting to you,
> achievable in the next 12 months and split into four
> categories—health, relationships, work/business and just
> for you.

IF THIS DOES NOT GET YOU DOWN TO FOUR GOALS, BECOME REALLY ruthless. You want to choose the goals that matter the most, that will compel you to achieve them. Choose four and sever the rest.

SMALL IS THE KEY TO IT ALL

Why did you go big just to go small? You brainstormed a massive wish list to get you actually thinking about what you want in life.

You cannot start to figure out HOW to get what you want until you are able to ascertain WHAT you want. Clarity is power.

Then you went small so you could invite your subconscious and the universe to come up with ideas to make your dreams into realities. This won't happen with a ton of ideas—the extreme focus is essential.

At this stage the goals don't have to be written well or look pretty. You will sort that out in the next chapter in which you are going to write out the goals in a way that makes them so engaging you can't help but be motivated to take action.

ACTION STEPS

Write down your goals wish list.

Select four goals from the list you want to tackle in the next 12 months.

8

WRITE YOUR FOUR SUPER SEXY GOALS

 'In the beginner's mind there are many possibilities but in the expert's there are few.' – Shunryu Suzuki

A Dirty Little Secret

Here is a secret I probably should have told you earlier. It doesn't really matter which four goals you choose. Yes they should be appealing, but don't worry if you don't feel as passionate about them as you think you should be. Do not stress if you don't think they are the most magnificent goals ever. Just choose four things you want. Pick four and be done with it.

Once you start taking action on these four goals and see them being accomplished, your belief that goal setting can have a positive, even profound impact on your life will be created. Four goals, no matter what they entail, no matter if they are big or small or purple or green gives you a better chance at seeing that the actions you take bring about fulfillment and success.

Next year you are much more likely to pull out that big wish list you put away and select four more goals to try and achieve. Goal setting then becomes a powerful habit in your life.

So pick four goals. Any four. Now you are going to write them out in a way that makes it impossible not to take action on them.

CHALLENGE YOURSELF

Another thing before we get into the nitty gritty of actually writing out your top four goals in the sexiest way possible. Now is a good time to look at your goals and decide if they are challenging enough but not too challenging.

The tip here is to lean towards making them more challenging than less. If you have written that you want to win an Olympic medal, play a violin solo at Carnegie Hall or take a rocket ship to Mars, then you may want to scale that goal back. You only have one year!

But if your goals don't give you a jittery feeling, then aim a bit higher. If you don't achieve that exact perfect end goal, you will have likely achieved more than you would have done otherwise. You have written half of a novel? Great, you have gone further than most people.

When a goal is slightly beyond what you consider achievable, it forces you to work out ways to make it possible. More on this later, but you can ask others to help, or commit yourself fully to your goal for a set period, or find a person who has achieved what you want and mimic them. You will be surprised how much you can accomplish in just one year.

THREE TYPES OF GOALS

You have likely written your goals in one of three ways:

END GOAL

This is the final piece of the puzzle or rung of the ladder. It is what makes the goal feel complete, a success. For example: win a marathon, write a New York Times best seller or watch a spectacular sunset over Maui. These paint a great picture of goal completion, but the trouble is that the final step of the goal is out of your hands. You may be running against an Olympian, publish your book on the same day as a new Harry Potter or visit Maui in rainy season. You can use parts of this end goal picture in your goal writing, but don't rely on it to feel like you have successfully completed the goal. After all, winning the lottery can be a goal, but if it is out of your hands to succeed at it, it becomes rather meaningless.

PERFORMANCE GOAL

This is describing what you would like to achieve when you finish the goal. It is slightly different from above as it is mostly within your control. For example: complete the marathon in a certain time frame, publish the book and get in the top ten in an Amazon category, have a cocktail on the beach in Maui. It may seem slightly less exciting than an end goal above, but it makes for a compelling and attainable goal.

PROCESS GOAL

This tells you what you have to do to achieve the goal. Effectively these can be thought of as the actions you take, or the habits you build or mini-goals. For example: run 10 miles three times per week, write at least 1000 words every day, save a certain amount of money each week for the trip to Maui. When you are writing out your ultimate goal, you will exclude these, but they become important when you are writing your action plan, which is covered in the next chapter.

Super Sexy Elements

A super sexy goal has three elements: powerful language, a vivid description and an emotional connection weaved in. Let us look at these parts of the written goal in a bit more detail.

Powerful Language

Be very clear and specific about what you want. State the goal in the positive, use action words and include an exact deadline. Be concise—one or two sentences are enough.

Vivid Description

Create a brief description that conveys in an action replay type way exactly what you will be doing when your goal is reached. Super sexy tip—if you can't imagine it, then think about the Facebook status update you will write. When I decided to do the fire walk, I couldn't begin to imagine what the whole experience would be like, but I knew I could write 'I am now a firewalker' on Facebook.

Emotion and Meaning

Weave into the short, powerful, vivid description the meaning the goal has for you—why you will feel so happy or successful or excited when you achieve it. Add a sprinkle of emotion—your exact feelings as your goal is reached. This is all tied in with your 'why', your purpose that will be fleshed out with the action steps later. But for now, add a taste of your emotional connection to the goal.

THIS MAY SEEM LIKE A LOT TO PACK INTO A COUPLE OF SENTENCES, but it is really simple if you use the following templates.

TEMPLATES AND EXAMPLES

Here are two super sexy templates that I use to write goals that carry all these elements. Pick what resonates with you, get your four goals and rewrite them using the templates and examples below. Remember only do this with your top four goals. You will run out of steam if you try to do this with the entire goals wish list.

It is (future date) and I am/ I have (end step). I am feeling...

I am so happy and grateful that (goal success) on or before (date). [Vivid description of goal].

HERE ARE SOME EXAMPLES OF MY OWN GOALS USING THE TEMPLATES above:

It is November 2008 and I have just completed the Auckland half marathon in less than 2 ½ hours. I am feeling great and my support team is patting me on the back and telling me well done.

It is October 2015 and I have just sold the very first copy of my first book. I am feeling excited as I know this is just the beginning of a new way to earn income.

It is the end of July 2017 and I have just stood on the scales ten pounds lighter than the start of the year. I am a lot more energized with my focus on exercise and healthy eating.

I am so happy and grateful that I have bought my first investment property on or before March 2009. I am standing in the empty house, thinking this is all mine, and opening a bottle of champagne.

I am so happy and grateful that I travelled around Croatia on or before September 2010. I am lying on the beach in sun-drenched Croatia and reading a fantastic book, just relaxing and enjoying the sun.

I am so happy and grateful that I have published a children's picture book on or before October 2017. I have just received the first five-star review of my beautiful book and am feeling so happy that it is out in the world for kids and their parents to enjoy.

ONE YEAR, FOUR GOALS

Here is one illustration of four super sexy goals using the templates in the suggested categories—health, relationships, work, and 'just for you'.

> Health: I am so happy and grateful that I am more fit than I have been in the past five years on or before July 2018. I have just completed a gym workout and am feeling fit, strong, toned and full of energy.

> Relationship: It is August 2018 and I am on the eighth date of this year with my husband. We are out at our favorite local restaurant talking and laughing and feeling more connected than ever.

> Work/Business: I am so happy and grateful that I have published three Amazon best-selling books on or before October 2018. I have just taken a screen shot of my new book showing it is in the top 10 in its Amazon category.

> Just for You: It is the end of November 2018 and I am reading my new children's picture book to my son's class at school. I am feeling happy that I have produced something beautiful and fun for kids to enjoy.

The astute among you may have realized that I have just shared my top four super sexy goals for this year with you all! Everyone who reads this book can now hold me accountable. More on accountability soon.

Note that I didn't write a goal about my kids or my home or my friends. This does not imply that they are any less important in my day-to-day life. It is simply that there is not a goal around them for this year.

.   .   .

ANOTHER DIRTY LITTLE SECRET

Just because you write your goals in this way doesn't guarantee success. But it sure gives them more of a prospect. When a goal, any goal, achieves fruition, it is rather miraculous. If you attempt all four this year and only get one, isn't it still worth a try?

Writing down a goal that doesn't end up as the success you wanted is hard. Not writing down any goals and living an average life (broke and unhappy) is hard. Choose your hard.

> In summary: write out a brief, informative, emotionally-charged goal you would be happy to say out loud.

DO THIS BECAUSE YOU WANT YOUR GOALS TO BE SO IRRESISTIBLE that you cannot NOT tackle them. It is a no brainer to embark on them. Do this because you are creating a big enough reason to figure out the how. This how, this taking action, is covered in the next chapter.

ACTION STEP

Write down your four super sexy goals for the next 12 months using the templates.

9

TAKE ACTION (EAT ELEPHANTS AND FROGS)

 'The most effective way to do it, is to do it.' – Amelia Earhart

Nom Nom Nom

There seems to be an obsession with devouring animals in goal-setting literature. Breaking goals into small steps is depicted as eating an elephant 'one bite at a time'. We are told to 'eat that frog' when we tackle the hardest or most impactful task first.

Maybe taking action is described in metaphors because it is more romantic than thinking of all the hard work that is involved. Yes, taking action may be the least sexy part of super sexy goals, as you have to actually DO something. This chapter explains how this part can be, if not fun, at least easy and painless.

RPM

You have written a super sexy goal—a RESULT you want to see. You now want to add in the PURPOSE behind it and a MASSIVE ACTION PLAN. This RPM—Results, Purpose, Massive Action Plan method is recommended by author, coach and personal development expert, Tony Robbins. After 40 years of coaching everyone from people on the verge of suicide to presidents, he knows a thing or two about achieving goals, so why not try it?

Writing out the purpose or 'why' behind your goals gives you extra motivation to achieve them. Do not skip this step! It is where your emotional juice is. When the going gets tough, reading your why may be the only thing that gets you through. Move beyond the literal answer and get to how you want to feel.

The massive action plan is a big picture overview of the main actions to achieve your goal. It is the 'map'. These actions don't have to be in order, be prioritized or be scheduled. You will do this next. For now, it is about getting them down.

This is best illustrated in an example. Here are two of my previous goals written using the RPM method:

HEALTH

Goal (Result):

It is the end of July 2017 and I have just stood on the scales ten pounds lighter than the start of the year. I am a lot more energized with my focus on exercise and healthy eating.

Why? (Purpose):

- I have the strength and energy to do all the things I want to do
- What I put in my body is very important to my energy and wellbeing

How? (Massive Action Plan):

- Green drink – every weekday
- Go to the gym or for a walk every day
- Create a vegetarian dinner at least once per week
- No alcohol during the week
- No sugar after dinner
- Try a vegetable juice fast for at least one day
- Do the Color Run
- Do the Wanderlust 'triathlon'

WRITING - CHILDREN

Goal (Result):

I am so happy and grateful that I have published a children's picture book on or before October 2017. I have just received the first five-star review of my beautiful book.

Why? (Purpose):

- Fun to write something that kids will love
- Want to show that it is possible to self-publish a great picture book

How? (Massive Action Plan):

- Collate and format *Maxy Moo* book
- Get a book launch team together
- Launch the book out into the world
- Read book to local daycare

Notice that the number of bullet points varies. I could easily think of a lot of specific ways to get healthier, but as I had never produced a picture book before, the action steps involved were fewer and more vague.

Brainstorm a few reasons why you are embarking on each of the four goals and decide on a few of the main actions that you will take. Do not take ages on this; give yourself an hour or so at the most. You can change your reasons and action steps if they are not working for you. Just get something down so you can start prioritizing and scheduling.

Prioritizing

You now have a handful of action items, but what is the best one to do first? The trouble with a lot of goal setting books is that they tell you to write the goal and then formulate the whole action plan to achieve them. As if you would suddenly and immaculately know all the action steps in the right order to get the goal you want!

Actually it is better if you don't know. If I had known everything I would have to do to make that half marathon run happen, I don't think I would have attempted it. It is important to be able to work out some chunks of action when you write your goals, but for now you need to take the first step.

Most people have heard of Pareto's principle—the 80/20 rule— that 80% of results often come from 20% of actions or tasks. Think about what that 20% is for your goals. In fact, go even more focused than that. In Gary Keller and Jay Papasan's book *The One Thing,* it is stated that we should ask this powerful question:

'What is the ONE thing (right now) I can do such that by doing it everything else would be easier or unnecessary?'

It is extreme Pareto—the 20% of the 20% of the 20% to the single most important ONE thing. This identifies what they call the 'lead domino'. The domino at the start of the chain that creates a domino effect when it is pushed over. Figure out the 'lead domino' and then whack away at it until it falls and other dominos fall in sequence, too. Look, you may not know what this is, but take an educated guess. Listen to your intuition.

For my health goal last year this was eliminating sugar completely out of my diet. You will notice the action step in my original plan said no sugar after dinner, but at the start of May last year, I took processed sugar out of my diet completely. This led to more energy, to wanting to go for a walk or to the gym each day and to finding more healthy food alternatives, especially at snack time. For the children's picture book goal this was deciding to pay a designer to collate and format the book rather than doing it myself. That freed up my time for things I could do well, like gathering a launch team, and meant the book was ready in a shorter time and looked more beautiful than anything I could have produced on my own.

What is your ONE thing or lead domino action step for each of your four goals?

SCHEDULING

We are now at the pinnacle of the least sexy part of goal setting. Putting the most important action steps in your calendar. Don't run away now! You have come so far. First, it doesn't matter what sort of calendar or diary system you use—digital or traditional, daily, weekly, monthly, or yearly. Just get it in there.

Take a big picture view of the next 12 months with all your scheduled appointments and plans in your diary or calendar. Decide on when you will devote time to your goals and block out those times as well. You may want to block out 15 minutes each weekday or a half-day each weekend, for example.

Once you figure out your first tasks or 'lead dominos', add a short description into your blocked out times. This may be best just for the first month or two. Do not worry if you are not sure what the task is or how long it will take to finish it. Just shade out time. Treat it like another appointment and make yourself unavailable.

Then try to stick to your schedule. Yes, you may not get that task done in the time you have available, but you have started to 'eat the elephant'. And yes, life can take over—your child gets sick or you have an emergency dental appointment—but if you don't schedule it, it definitely won't happen. At least if it is in the diary or calendar, there is a likelihood of spending time on it.

Review on a daily, weekly or monthly basis. I find reviewing and rescheduling on a weekly basis best for me so I will detail this method. On Sunday evening I spend about 20 minutes looking at the week ahead. I put in my work, exercise, scheduled appointments, kids' activities and anything else that I know will happen. Then I work out one or two most important tasks from my Massive Action Plan and time block them. This can be 10 minutes to full days.

TOP TIPS TO TAKE ACTION

Here are six tips to help make choosing, prioritizing and scheduling actions even easier:

.   .   .

Give Up Something

Perhaps you are trying to be the 'busy champion of the world' and there is NO WAY you can squeeze in even taking one bite of the elephant into your already full to overflowing life. Give something up that keeps you playing small. It doesn't have to be forever, but give it up for a week and see if that helps. Stop watching the news every night; cancel that subscription to a magazine you never read, or change the notification settings on your social media accounts. You can do something about removing the superfluous busy things that do not add any value to your life. I have recently taken the Facebook app off my phone and it has stopped me from compulsively checking it many times a day. Essentially, you are sacrificing some instant gratification for an end goal that creates much more value ('sexiness') in your life. Believe me, it is worth it.

Use Your Calendar

Utilize your calendar or diary system in the best way possible. If there is ONE thing you want to get done today that moves you toward your goals, some people find that writing that on a Post-It note and placing it where they see it is helpful. Then you can rip the Post-It note off the computer or wall and scrunch it up in a burst of enthusiasm when that task is checked off. If you want to do something every day towards your goals (go for a walk, write 1,000 words, etc.), then get a wall calendar and 'don't break the chain'. Put a cross on the calendar for every day you take action and try to keep that chain of crosses going. I can't tell you how helpful 'don't break the chain' is for writing the first draft of a book.

. . .

Try an 'If-Then' Plan

If you are not sure exactly when you can assign time to a goal task for the week, then try an 'if-then' plan. This is spelled out in the excellent book, *Succeed* by Heidi Grant Halvorson. Tell yourself if your partner is taking your child to her sports game, then you will go for a run. But if you are taking her, then you can spend half the time of the game on writing your book. If you finish work late, you will commit to a ten-minute walk, but if you get out on time, you will go to that hour-long class at the gym.

Just Do One

Do one tiny little thing to start you off. Can't face 20 push-ups? Commit to doing just one. You have time for one push up. An old idea is to floss just one tooth. Give yourself permission to finish after one. You have taken the action you said you would take for the day. Usually you will continue, but you are a success in what you set out to do regardless.

Don't Eat that Frog

We are told to 'eat that frog'—do the hardest or most impactful task first. But sometimes eating that frog seems too daunting. So don't. Do a secondary task that doesn't exert as much willpower but still brings you closer to the goal. Invite people to join your book launch team instead of writing the next chapter. Walk instead of jog. Have date night in the living room instead of trying to dress up and find babysitters. Don't do this all the time, but if you are tired, then don't feel the need to over exert yourself. The last thing you want is to stop the momentum entirely. At least this way you can feel like you are doing something that moves you forward.

. . .

Kill Two Birds with One Stone

The absolute best tip is to work out some high-impact activities. Can you schedule something in that goes towards two or more goals at the same time? For instance, you could have a brisk game of tag outside with your children, thus checking off health (exercise) and relationships (quality time with kids).

Schedule Your Dreams

Dream big and then schedule your dreams. Sure, organization and time management don't seem sexy.

> Consistently choosing in favor of what you really want and feeling energized with a new purpose—now that IS sexy.

Just start. This creates a ripple effect. And when you are in motion you can see the next action step, the next domino. You are not as far away from your goals as you may think you are. It is not a big leap, but small changes—each tiny bite of the elephant— that bring even the most far-fetched goal into reach.

By now you may have encountered some issues with goals. This is good news as it means goal setting is working! The next chapter tackles three of the main problems you may face.

Action Steps

Write down your RPM plan for each of your four super sexy goals.

Work out the first thing to focus on ('the lead domino') for each of the goals.

Shade out some time in your diary or calendar to work on your goals.

Review your diary or calendar and your scheduled tasks on a consistent basis.

10

GOAL SETTING PROBLEMS AND SOLUTIONS

 'We are all in the gutter, but some of us are looking at the stars.' – Oscar Wilde

THE BAD NEWS

I have some bad news for you. Even with the most appealing and meaningful goals, the most focused commitment and the best prioritizing and scheduling structure for taking action, you WILL encounter problems. This system does everything in its power to set up the goals for the best chance at success, but it is important to realize that at times this won't be easy and you will have to learn to deal with issues along the way. Having goals does not eliminate problems, but hopefully it gives you better quality problems!

Here are three main goal-setting problems and some tips and tools to overcome them.

. . .

OBSTACLES

You are at the start of your goal. Day one. The first step. And way in the distance, around all those bends and over those hills and down through those valleys is your goal. With those many miles between you and your goal, it is obvious that there will be obstacles on the way to achieving it.

Most people don't set goals. I understand that. But then, unfortunately, of the small number of people who embark on goals, many give them up at the first major hurdle.

Obstacles can come in many different forms and be in all areas—from limitations in money, resources and time, to loved ones being negative about the goal. What happens when people encounter obstacles? Often they stop or go back, or even more ridiculously, but very commonly, they carry the obstacle around with them as some sort of 'proof' that they shouldn't be going for the goal!

You have a car breakdown that wipes out all your travel savings. Or you have a fight with your spouse on your first date night in two years, or a dog chases you on your morning run. So you tell yourself that it was not meant to be or it is too ambitious or ask, 'Who am I to want something like that?'

No matter what type of obstacle you encounter, the first thing that needs to change is your beliefs about obstacles. Your mindset in this area needs a complete overhaul if you are ever going to succeed in your goals.

Obstacles are actually fan-flippin-tastic!

You WANT to have obstacles! Obstacles don't exist until you set goals, and they only start to show up when you are on the way to achieving your goals. So you should get really excited, as they show you that goal setting works—it is taking you somewhere.

Here are some tips on overcoming obstacles. When you first set a goal, studies have proven that the best mindset is to be positive about success but not about how easy it will be. You need to be positive that it will be tough and there will be obstacles. You don't have to know (and won't know) every obstacle in advance, but you can prepare for some of them. When I ran the half-marathon I knew my feet needed extra care and I spent money on appropriate footwear and podiatrist visits. Just know that in your head you will have a kind of mental contrast in which you hold onto the positivity of how it will be when you achieve the goal and also maintain realistic thoughts about what it will really take to get there.

Flexibility is the key to goal setting. You don't expect to move in a straight line anywhere else in life, so why would goal setting be any different? Adjustments and course corrections will be required. If your environment doesn't support your goals, what can you do to change your environment? Can you sell your unreliable car and take public transport, go to the movies with your spouse instead of talking over dinner or run along a different route?

One major obstacle many people encounter is negative reactions from others. Remember what was said earlier in the objections chapter. You OWE it to the world to use the gifts and resources you have been bestowed. Otherwise you have been given the golden ticket and thrown it away.

You may be worried about how all this change is going to affect your loved ones. Honestly, if you don't tell them about your goals, at least not straight away, your partner, kids, family and friends may not notice at all. If there is a comment or even friction, explain that you are working on becoming a better person. Tell them you are going to be the same person but more YOU: less distracted, less stressed, happier and more fun. How could anyone say they wouldn't like that? If there is still some conflict, realize that their reactions are just coming from their own needs, and you have the power to respond in the most resourceful way you can.

You may still be wondering how to tackle a specific obstacle that has arisen. Overcoming obstacles is a muscle that you need to build up. The more you do it, the easier it will be. As long as you frame obstacles as a good thing, you are halfway there already.

WHEN TO GIVE UP?

How to choose whether to give up or keep going with a goal can be a big issue in goal setting. But the answer to this is simple. IF and only if the goal is costing you too much—in that it doesn't reflect the real you, is causing significant sacrifice in most other areas of your life, is taking up all your time with no end in sight, or is making you deeply unhappy or unwell—can you give it up. That is it.

Too big a sacrifice means give up. If you don't want to do a particularly unpleasant but necessary action step of a goal, or if you encounter any other obstacle, no matter how enormous, keep going.

My friend Barry took on an incredible goal at the start of last year —he planned to hike up to Mount Everest basecamp in Nepal, over 5,300m or 17,500 feet above sea level. Unfortunately, seven days into the trek, Barry developed a lung infection caused by the freezing temperatures. That combined with mild food poisoning meant that he had to make the difficult decision not to continue. He was at Gorak-Shep, over 5,000m or almost 17,000 feet above sea level, less than a three-hour hike from Everest basecamp.

You would perhaps think that he would be devastated by not achieving his ultimate goal, but he is actually on cloud nine about the whole experience. He does not regret a single thing. He is amazed with his mental fortitude—he says he climbed with his mind, not his legs. He became better at decision making and overcoming unexpected challenges. He is pleased with what his body could handle—even in dusty or freezing conditions. He got closer to his hiking club friends who came on the trip, and at 51 is fitter than he has ever been. Plus he felt a profound sense of being alive in the magnificent mountain landscape.

> Set some goals because even if you give up on them, they
> will likely have a lasting impact on your life.

One thing you should contemplate up front is how much of a 'follow through' kind of person you are. Some people do about 80% of something and then delegate the rest or decide it is good enough to be thought of as finished. Others have to dot every I and cross every T to feel done. Knowing how well you follow through will help you decide if this giving up idea is just a pattern that repeats a lot in your life—one that may not serve you all that well.

When you are on the road to improving a skill or mastering something, everyone gets a burst of progress and then a plateau. You will get stronger in your new fitness regime but then not change weights for a while. You will get a couple of quick promotions and then not move upwards for ages. The most successful people know that the plateau is just a stage in the goal and not a reason to give up. They will look at alternative ways to move past the plateau to another growth period, even if it means going sideways or backwards for a bit. Learn to respect the plateau stage, as it is part of the mastery.

Sometimes people put a lot of hard work into a goal only to realize they are too far down the wrong path and have to give up. The key to making sure this doesn't happen is to regularly review your goals. Check in with whether you are in the right place and course correct as necessary. This is failing on a small scale; failing forward, and hopefully will avoid a big 'Should I give up?' later on. You may feel that if you stop to check how you are doing, you will lose momentum or get some feedback you don't want, but this is a lesser issue than proceeding in the wrong direction until you reach a destination you did not want to visit.

If you give up on a goal, focus on the other three goals, and if it works, add a new goal into the mix. Please don't give up on all your goals if one doesn't work out.

COMPETING GOALS

One major way you can trip yourself up is to have competing goals. You help this by first being aware that it can be an issue. Many people don't even think about it. You can also try to decide on goals that complement each other when you brainstorm and write them. And as noted in the previous chapter, you can stack actions to check off more than one goal at a time. But at times goals will compete for your attention and resources; it is baked into your busy life, so what do you do about this problem?

First, understand that a balanced life is a myth. Extraordinary results require focused attention and time, and that means time away from other things, so that makes balance impossible.

If you have a looming deadline, know that sometimes one goal will take priority for a while. Whatever you do, do NOT neglect your health for too long—healthy food, exercise and enough sleep are critical—or ALL your goals will fall down.

Most importantly, if your self-control reserves are low, don't pursue two goals at once that both require a lot of self-control. If you want to write a novel and run a marathon in the same year and you have done neither before, then consider concentrating on one in the first half of the year and the other in the second half, for example, rather than both of them for the entire 12 months.

Having no more than four goals will help to reduce the chance of competing goals and goal overwhelm in general. If it helps, only focus on one, two or three goals, at least for a time. Knowing that goal conflicts are a common issue and they are not an excuse to give up or fail at your goals should also help considerably.

Having conflicting goals is hard at times. Having no goals at all because of a goal conflict and staying in your average life is hard. Choose your hard.

The Good News

When you step out of your comfort zone and strive to reach your potential you will encounter mess. Being okay with chaos is an essential element of successfully completing goals.

Breathe through the chaos.

Remember your Lizard mind is not used to all this positive action and progressing forward. It likes you to stay tucked up in your little comfort zone. It bombards you with negative thinking that any problem automatically means goal failure and necessitates retreat.

You now have everything you need to successfully counter Lizard thinking. Well-written, vividly-painted and emotionally-charged goals. Reasons why your goals will bring you fulfillment and success. Action steps with ways to prioritize and schedule tasks. Plus ways to handle the main goal-setting problems that arise.

You have no excuses—start on your goals today!

A few strategies to guarantee goal success are covered in the next chapter. This is the penultimate chapter before we wrap everything up in one last sexy chapter.

11

SUPERCHARGE YOUR SUPER SEXY GOALS

 'Instead of wondering when our next vacation is, we should set up a life we don't need to escape from.' – Seth Godin

META GOAL

I can't tell you how much deadlines, rewards and accountability helped in finishing writing the first draft of this book. I told everyone my plan to finish the first draft before Christmas and then take a few days off over the festive season as a reward of sorts. After all, it almost seems compulsory to have a goal when you are writing a book on goal setting!

Sure, the Christmas deadline was of my own making. Sure, I could have still worked on it over the festive break. And sure, not many people would hold me accountable as most people are rushing around at Christmas time and are unlikely to remember what I said in passing about writing a book.

But these three strategies directed my attention to the most important thing for me—getting the first draft of this book written. I gave up things, I delegated, and I stayed up a little later than I normally would. But I achieved my goal. And it felt pretty darn good.

You will encounter problems when going for your goals, but you also have a lot of power to do everything you can to make them happen. Here are nine top tools that will help you achieve your super sexy goals.

DEADLINES

Everyone has experienced the power of a deadline at some stage in his or her life. From a due date on an essay to a work project, having a deadline makes it easier to aim at something. As noted above they can be artificial—a date you have plucked out that seems like a reasonable time by which to get your goal done. Or they can be imposed from the outside—a triathlon race date for example.

The most important thing to remember with deadlines is to not beat yourself up too much if you don't hit them. Don't give yourself a pass to let them fly by every single time, but if you have to move the goal posts, it is not usually the end of the world.

Especially if it is something you haven't done before, you may only have a vague notion of the effort it can take. I thought it would take two months to publish my children's picture book, *Maxy-Moo Flies to the Moon*. Instead it took me close to two years to get it out into the world. It was still worth it in the end, and in fact, the long anticipation of seeing that goal come to fruition made the book launch even better.

Sometimes, when you achieve a goal before the looming deadline hits, you feel like a rock star. This is particularly true if it seems impossible. National Novel Writing Month (NaNoWriMo) challenges people to write a 50,000-word (approximately 200-page) novel in a month. When I signed up for the challenge I thought there was no chance I would accomplish such a feat in such a short amount of time. I got to 50,000 words with a couple of days to spare. Sure, my silly romance is unlikely to be published in its current state, but I wrote a novel and not everyone can say that.

The super sexy goal setting system gives you 12 months to complete your goals. This is arbitrary, but it is a finite period in which you can achieve something worthy. Sometimes it is better to make the deadline shorter rather than longer as you don't strive for perfection or procrastinate and just actually finish something. Overall, though, if you get somewhere, anywhere on the journey to your ultimate goal before your deadline, it is better than not doing anything.

REWARDS

Rewards and incentives, when used in the right way, can be a very powerful method to aid in enjoying each step to accomplishing a goal.

In theory at least, internal drivers are much more important than external rewards. There are three keys for keeping motivation high: knowing the purpose behind the task, mastery of the task and autonomy (control over the task). Remember pull motivation? You want to have some of this baked into the goals you have set so they are intrinsically rewarding.

Sometimes you just need a bit more help, so what else can you do? Use push motivation methods. Have a built-in celebration system. Celebrate in small ways any task completed or mini goal achieved. Pat yourself on the back, indulge in some rest time or take a walk in the sunshine.

For bigger milestones amp up the rewards. This is especially important when you have had to do something very challenging or difficult and the intrinsic rewards have dried up. Go out for dinner, buy yourself some flowers or indulge in that latest binge-watching sensation. Do something nice for yourself. It is best if you don't rely on this method; only do it occasionally so you can feel like it is an unexpected benefit.

Of course, we should all be falling in love with the journey as well as the dream goal. So constantly ask yourself how you can make the action more fun or enjoyable. Remember, this is what successful people do. Run on the treadmill while listening to your favorite podcast. Or keep a gratitude journal about your goals and life. Savor how much getting to the end of something means to you by taking a photo of the occasion or bragging to someone about it. If you keep up a positive attitude, the whole thing is a win no matter what.

ACCOUNTABILITY

Telling people about your goals can have its downsides if done incorrectly, but done right it can improve your chances of success by up to 80%, or twice as much as just writing them down, depending on which study you read.

Two things you must be aware of before you share your goals. First, choose people who are more likely to support your goals. Being an accountability partner for someone requires time and effort, so choose him or her wisely. You want someone who gives you attention, motivation, information, inspiration, feedback and expertise. Look to friends who have achieved similar goals or be prepared to pay for a mentor or a coach.

In addition, share your goal in a way that makes your brain think you still have to actually do the goal. As entrepreneur and author, Derek Sivers, notes in his short TEDx talk 'Keep your goals to yourself', you need to have a future tense way of stating the goal, otherwise your mind thinks the goal is done and releases the tension required to take action. Don't tell people that you are running a marathon race soon. Rephrase it: 'I really need to train for this upcoming marathon'.

Decide on the best way to update your accountability partners— a daily text, a weekly Skype session or a monthly email update— and then commit to that. Tell them what you want from them, what questions they should ask and what they should follow up on. Be prepared to hear not just support and encouragement but hard truths and constructive criticism. They are not friends in this capacity; they are your accountability partners.

If you don't want to tell people what you are doing, you can find other ways to hold yourself accountable. Use a journal to log your progress. Or keep an anonymous profile on a site like stickk.com, which gives you options of rewards for achieving or punishments for not achieving your goals. You can program into stickk.com that you will donate money to a charity you don't like or give money to some of your friends if you don't get to your goal by your deadline. The 'carrot' method of using rewards combined with a literal stick method at stickk.com can work extremely well.

Review Your Goals Regularly

Deadlines, rewards and accountability are the three main tools I used to write this very book, but there are plenty of other tools that you can use to supercharge your goal success.

Make sure you have your super sexy goals list somewhere you have easy access to it and see it every day. Use a pen and paper version or print it out and stick it to your wall, on the fridge or on the bathroom mirror. For those who are more private, stick it inside the door to your wardrobe or tuck it into a journal you write in regularly. One pro tip is to sign your name at the bottom of the list. This seems silly, but it makes it a contract with yourself and somehow this makes it seem more legitimate.

If you have an electronic Word document or PDF of your list, then place that document on your computer desktop, or add it into your notes or books apps on your phone so you can open it up and read it regularly.

Some of you may want to share your goals list on your favorite social media feed, on Pinterest or on your own blog. Sharing it and getting others involved keeps you even more accountable, but as noted above, it does have a potential downside in that some people may be less than enthusiastic about your new pursuits.

A fun and completely optional way to display your goals list is to create a 'vision board' of it. A vision board is any sort of board on which you display images that represent your goals list items— what you want to do, see and master. Create one the old-fashioned way out of cut outs from magazines stuck to a big piece of paper or cardboard. Or combine some pictures into an online board on Pinterest or elsewhere.

An extra cool idea is to take a photo of your written goals list or its physical vision board and upload it so it becomes your computer screen saver or wallpaper on your phone. We look at our phones on average over 100 times a day, so the goals list will be reviewed, at least subconsciously, an enormous amount.

Alternatively, be more active in reviewing your goals. Ask yourself powerful questions such as 'what is one thing I can do today to help me achieve this goal?' Recite the goals as affirmations in a confident voice. Read the goal then close your eyes and visualize what the scene will be like when it is achieved. Bask in that visualization for a few moments.

Choose to read, review and display your goals list in a way that reflects you. The point is to not forget your goals. They will become more real the more you review them and then you are more likely to take action.

ROLE MODELS

Goals are particularly difficult when you are embarking on something you have never done before. One way to help with this is to find someone who is doing or has already achieved what you want and use them as a role model. This can be a real-life friend, someone in a book you read, a famous person whom you look up to or a coach. You want to find someone who is successful at what you want to do. You will be amazed at how much information you can find out about their strategies just from reading books or articles or searching online.

Channeling role models helps you shift your identity. It makes you think about the person you want to BE rather than just what you want to DO. Take some of your role model's determination or strength or grace as well as their strategies and utilize it for your own benefit.

> We don't get our goals, we get who we think we are.

One caveat here is to work at your own pace and reach the goal you want. If someone you are modeling is out of this world successful, you may never reach that level. But if you move to attain even one percent of their success, then you are ahead of where you were, and that is the only thing that is important. Play your own game, no one else's.

Say NO

It has already been mentioned that you will have to give up stuff to make way for your goals. This can be as easy as turning off the news or Twitter for a while, but sometimes when you say 'no' you have to say it directly. Saying 'no' politely but assertively is a powerful time management skill. Here are a few ways to say 'no' nicely:

> 'Sounds wonderful, but that is not part of my work focus right now.'
> 'Sorry but my current commitments mean I cannot take that on.'
> 'It sounds amazing but I wouldn't be able to give that the attention it deserves.'
> 'I can't help you right now but can schedule it after X date.'

Another way to say 'no' is to call it a policy: 'Sorry it is not my policy to do (such and such)'. People respect policies, even ones you have made up yourself, and you just said 'no' without even actually saying no!

Even in the nicest way possible, saying 'no' is uncomfortable so practice on small things and build up.

> If you do not learn to say 'no', then you are saying YES to someone else's agenda and NO to yourself.

You will know in your gut if 'no' is the right answer. If you are unsure, give it the 'Hell Yeah!' test. As Derek Sivers (quoted twice in the same chapter, lucky him) says, 'if it's not a hell yeah, it is a NO'.

If a 'no' is done well, people should be happy with how clear you are and how committed you are to what is important to you. And, well, if they are not, too bad. Their response is their problem.

ROUTINES

Having goals sets you up for a large amount of decision making and mental strain. You may not be able to get out of the extra stamina required to attain goals, but you can take out any extra energy from other parts of your life so you don't feel overwhelmed.

Having the same routine is one way to spend less energy on things that are not as important as your goals and if done right also makes sure you look after your personal wellbeing. A good routine is to go to bed at the same time each night. Some successful people take this further and have the same thing for breakfast each morning or wear similar outfits every day.

Another way to build routine into goal setting is to have triggers or anchors that create an environment that the goal task is underway. I have a classical music playlist and when I put those headphones on, I know it is book-writing time.

GO HARD AT FIRST

Personal development expert, Tony Robbins, states that the path to mastery starts with a period of total immersion then continues with scheduled repetition. He asserts that if you commit to doing something just five times in a row, such as going to the gym every day, this will create momentum and you will continue with it. So if you want to learn something new, then go to the dance or painting or judo class every night for a week or commit to at least ten lessons in one month. After that scale it back.

This period of intensity is temporary, just enough to convert your willpower into a positive habit. Success can be thought of as a sprint fueled by discipline just long enough for habit to kick in and take over. When you see disciplined people, you are really seeing people who have trained a handful of powerful habits into their lives, usually by this immersion technique.

During this intense stage of learning really lean into your support network. Delegate or eliminate what is not important for this limited time in your life. Ask your spouse to cook or pay for a meal delivery service. Get your kids to do chores or pay for a cleaner. Do whatever it takes to get past that first uncertain stage of skill building and then work at a less reckless pace from there.

This may seem contradictory to the 'just do one small thing' advice earlier, but it is not. Taking small actions is for when you need to keep going but may be worn out by day-to-day tasks. Going hard is for when you are in the initial stages of your goal and you are still incredibly motivated and excited.

Have Fun

Fun is not just a 'nice to have' but also an essential part of goal setting. Studies have shown that incorporating fun into goals not only increases satisfaction but actual performance of the goal by a considerable amount.

Don't worry that scheduling fun stops it being fun. Fun is fun and we all need more of it. If that means being less spontaneous by blocking out time for it, then that is what is required.

Fortunately, fun is woven into the fabric of the super sexy goal system, as there is a goal just for you that should be at least a little fun, even if it is a challenge as well. In addition, an emphasis on enjoyment is now part of your new mindset around goals. After all, successful people constantly ask 'how can I enjoy this?' and resolve to remain positive about tasks that the average person doesn't like and want to do.

Include fun in your life outside of your goals, have it as a part of the 'just for you' goal, enjoy checking off your goals and strive to be positive on the journey towards them. Simply, have fun.

CHERRY ON THE TOP

These are really powerful tools that are the cherry on the top of an already robust and sexy goal-setting system. Just know they are there and can be retrieved from the toolbox when required.

12

THE REAL GOAL OF THIS BOOK

 'What you get by achieving your goals is not as important as what you become by achieving your goals.'
– Henry David Thoreau

THIS BOOK IS A SUCCESS IF...

Getting a goal is about stepping out of your comfort zone, facing your fears and going for it. If you take action, any action at all, despite your fear, then this book is a success.

Goal setting is a system for you to stop the busy overwhelm that leads to nowhere. It is a way to be clear in your life and to bat away distractions easily. It is a tool to allow you to pinpoint what you want so you can say no to things that add no value to your life. Even if you never attain any of your goals, but you pick up these skills, then this book is a success.

Taking action on goals means not conforming to society's expectations. It means quietly leaning into the whispers of what your soul truly desires and doing what is important to you. If you start rebelliously doing what you actually want to do, then this book is a success.

Writing goals is about gaining some insight, connecting with your true self and rediscovering what you desire from your life. You figure out what your strengths are and how you can use them to build a great life for you and your loved ones. It is not about changing but becoming more yourself. If you find that you are now more in touch with your authentic self, then this book is a success.

If this book has made you question your beliefs and changed your mindset around what you are capable of, then this book is, without a doubt, a success.

Happiness

Throughout this book I promised that goals will make you feel successful or accomplished or fulfilled, but I didn't promise that it would directly lead to happiness. Happiness can be attained in the most fleeting of pleasures such as the sun on your face or a child's smile.

Succeeding at something hard often gives a greater satisfaction. Working out who you are at your best improves your confidence and self-esteem. Getting stronger—in your health, mental ability and improved potential makes you proud, and being proud is a huge source of happiness.

Life is not designed to be easy, but to present you with a series of challenges to help you grow. It is growth rather than the goal that is the ultimate prize. As motivational speaker, Jim Rohn advises, 'You want to set a goal that is big enough that in the process of achieving it, you become someone worth becoming'.

Happiness is a byproduct of figuring out a meaningful life. It is a result of doing positive things that improve your life. Don't aim for happiness, aim to grow. Aim for mastery. Aim for a life well lived, not pleasantly existed.

> Live a life in which you work hard to be fulfilled and successful, and you will experience a deeper level of happiness than you ever thought possible.

GOAL SETTING REVOLUTION

Motivating people to set and get goals has been the entire point of this book because I want to fire up the world and create a goal-setting revolution! I want to dramatically increase the number of people who write goals and actively strive to achieve them.

I know goal setting is not a panacea for all the world's woes. But I am certain that if more people embraced goals, we would have more outstanding and less average people in the world. More fit, wealthy and happy people ready to share their skills and creativity to bring more love and abundance to their communities.

But deep down that is not the aim of this book.

The real goal of this book is to get you to do something.

Do

Dream big and make every piece of your life the masterpiece it is meant to be because no matter how great your life is, there is another level—one of passion, gratitude, connection, joy and success.

Go beyond expectations and what you think you are capable of and the world opens up. You will discover there is so much more you can do with your mind, body, skills and talents. You may even compel others to dream big and focus on their goals, too.

And if dreaming big still seems too much, then know that modest goals on which you take action are better than aspirational dreams you do nothing about.

By now you have worked out that it doesn't matter really what goals you choose to pursue. At the very least you have some insight about yourself, have a bit of fun, learn skills you will have with you forever and possibly inspire others to live better.

Isn't that what life is all about?

So please, please, please do something. Do something different. Do something outside your comfort zone. Do something despite the fear.

Just DO.

Take action on one of your super sexy goals today.

— A *NOURISH YOUR SOUL* BOOK —

FIND YOUR PURPOSE
IN 15 MINUTES

YOUR SHORTCUT TO A
MEANINGFUL LIFE

JULIE SCHOOLER

FIND YOUR PURPOSE IN 15 MINUTES

Your Shortcut to a Meaningful Life

-A *Nourish Your Soul* Book-

Julie Schooler

CONTENTS

1. Despair to Delight   205
2. Why Are You Here?   213
3. Purpose Questions (and a Wee Rant)   223
4. Purpose Answers   229
5. Find Your Purpose in 15 Minutes   239
6. Plant Your Purpose in Your Mind, Heart and Soul   249
7. Purpose in the Real World   257
8. Diving Deeper: Tests   265
9. Diving Deeper: Questions   277
10. Diving Deeper: Exercises   285
11. Supercharge Your Purpose   293
12. What is the Purpose of a Book on Purpose?   299

  Appendix One – Find Your Purpose in 15 Minutes   303
  Summary
  Appendix Two – My Test Results   309
  Appendix Three – My Obituary Exercise   311

1
―――――

DESPAIR TO DELIGHT

 'Tell me, what is it you plan to do with your one wild and precious life?' – Mary Oliver

THE WORLD IS ON FIRE

- Do you feel like your life is going nowhere?
- Do you struggle to get out of bed each morning?
- Do you want your life be meaningful but don't know where to start?

More than ever, people all over the world are feeling disillusioned and disempowered. In Western countries many of us are fortunate to have plenty of material comforts, but statistics show that we are unhappier than we have ever been.

We are told that finding our purpose, our WHY, is the solution to thinking life is pointless. It is declared that discovering the meaning of our lives can help us feel less lost, eliminate our feelings of despair and make our day-to-day lives full of hope instead of drudgery.

BUT...

Finding a purpose looks too difficult to do, seems to take forever to work out and implies that our whole lives will have to change even if we somehow do manage to attempt this arduous task.

We are STUCK as we know we can't go on living this way without a purpose, BUT we are not sure how to find one.

No wonder the world feels like it is at a crisis point. No wonder we all eat too much, sit too much and binge watch too much. It's amazing that anyone gets out of bed in the morning at all!

The Purpose Solution

Find Your Purpose in 15 Minutes delivers a handy tool to help you discover your ideal life purpose in a matter of minutes.

This book will give you:

- A definition for purpose that is simple to understand and start from
- An easy-to-use template to write out your ideal purpose statement
- A 15-minute exercise that creates your purpose step-by-step
- An ideal purpose that feels profoundly significant and unique to you

You will not only find your purpose but also learn how to use it in your life. You will learn ways to LIVE it even if you don't know where to start or are afraid of change. This book will give strategies to help you to incorporate your newfound purpose seamlessly into your life and effortlessly stay the course.

This entertaining and easy-to-read guide will also cut through the confusion around what meaning, purpose, destiny and 'a calling' really are, provide compelling reasons why finding your purpose adds an uplifting element to your life and tells you exactly what to do to supercharge your purpose—even if you have never thought about any of these aspects before. If you enjoy the quick introspection during the purpose exercise, there is also the option of doing some extra tests, questions and exercises that help you understand and appreciate yourself on a deeper level.

You won't need to spend hours searching for information all over the Internet. You will have a clear direction and won't be confused by conflicting advice. This book will give you the exact blueprint to writing your own purpose in a way that feels like you have known it all along. Your purpose will help you spring out of bed every morning with renewed enthusiasm for living, not just existing.

How Finding My Purpose Helps YOU

Like you, I want my life to feel meaningful and worthwhile, so I spent a long, long time trying to figure out my ultimate purpose. I read lots of books, researched the topic extensively and went to many motivational seminars and personal development events.

I thought that something this significant should take serious contemplation plus long hours trying to understand my intuitive desires, childhood wishes and visions of my ideal future.

BUT....

Recently I had an epiphany: why does it need to be so difficult?

The more important thing is LIVING with purpose. If I could just eliminate the so-called hard part of working it out, I could swiftly start maneuvering my life in the right direction.

I distilled the avalanche of information and all my learnings into a simple and fun fool-proof formula to find my purpose. Then I got on with the more important job: starting to live it.

Finding my purpose in 15 minutes helped me to structure my life better, say 'no' to the unimportant and feel renewed energy when the perfect project for me came my way. It gave me clarity, simplicity and freedom. I find it amazing that one short statement can convey so much power.

It was obvious to me that many people could use this life shortcut to help them with both their day-to-day and their big picture decisions so they too could feel like they were working towards a destiny.

I could not find one short, clear, gimmick-free guide on how to find your purpose in this way, so I wrote one. This book contains all the tools, advice and inspiration you need to find and live your purpose in a way that makes your heart sing.

I have written the book that I wanted to read.

Purpose Rewards

Just think how great it will be when you find your purpose in 15 minutes. There are benefits in so many areas. You will:

- understand your true self better
- rediscover buried desires and drivers
- feel good about yourself for having a clear path
- know the direction to follow to get what you want
- lead and inspire others to live life on their own terms

- wake up each morning with a sense of excitement and zest for life
- feel like you are living the life you were meant to live, one with meaning and true joy

PURPOSE PRAISE

Busy people are happy to recommend this book as it contains everything they need and nothing they don't to easily discover their purpose in life. They are excited that there is a finally a short book that helps them to effortlessly write and take action on a clear meaning for their lives.

Readers are excited that there is finally a fun and easy-to-read book that removes any stigma that finding your purpose has to be serious, take a long time or that your life has to change in a dramatic way.

Early volunteers who took the 'Find Your Purpose in 15 Minutes' questionnaire had overwhelmingly positive feedback. They loved the opportunity to take some time to reflect on their lives, found the exercise short and sweet and were surprised something so simple could feel so profound. Many said they felt uplifted, empowered and inspired to live well.

This is just one of many amazing comments: "This is very insightful and I wish I had done it a long time ago. It's comforting and liberating at the same time. It makes all the noise fall away and provides that clarity we are always looking to find."

PURPOSE PROMISE

This book will make it exciting and easy to rediscover your purpose. This is the most stress-free and light-hearted book on finding your purpose you will ever read.

You will write your purpose so clearly and ingrain it so deeply you can recite it in your sleep. Plus it will get you bouncing with a joy of life you had forgotten you had.

In addition, I promise that you will have simple yet uplifting tools for bringing your life in line with your purpose without having to sell your house, ditch your family or move to a mountain in Nepal!

It is guaranteed that if you use this book to write your purpose, you will feel enthused about life once again, you will have less to worry about, and you will give yourself the best gift of all—a clear path to designing your destiny.

Find Your Purpose Today

Do not wait until you snooze another alarm clock buzzer over and over as you struggle to get out of bed. Read this book and add some much needed clarity, direction and fun back into your life. Find your purpose so you can immediately start to improve your health, relationships and work. Why postpone being happier?

A Simple Way to Shine

Find Your Purpose in 15 Minutes plucks out what is important to you, what you love, what you are good at and what you can give and easily inputs them into an ideal purpose statement just for you.

This book proves that finding your purpose - your WHY - can be fun, quick and simple. It CAN be a delight, if you let it. Plus it confirms how enriching it can be to weave your purpose into your life. Why not give yourself the gift of finding YOUR purpose today?

There is a light inside of you that has been dimmed for far too long.

Let the world see you shine.

2

WHY ARE YOU HERE?

 'Why stop now just when I'm hating it?' – Marvin, the paranoid android from *The Hitchhiker's Guide to the Galaxy*

The Answers

For thousands of years people have been asking questions centered on purpose: "What is the meaning of life?", "Why are we here?", "What is the purpose of MY life?".

The answers to these questions are even more varied than the questions themselves. They can be found amongst the ideas of ancient philosophers, in scientific theories, part of faith-based beliefs and even in popular culture.

Philosopher, Aristotle, fundamentally linked happiness to the meaning of life. Astrophysicist, Neil deGrasse Tyson says we create our own meaning, and many faith-based explanations associate a meaningful life with a relationship to a higher power.

Pop culture has even added its two cents: in the *Hitchhiker's Guide to the Galaxy* book series, the main characters finally discover the "answer to the ultimate question of life, the universe and everything" is, bizarrely, 42.

And no summary of questions and answers about purpose can be complete without this gem from the Monty Python film, *The Meaning of Life*, in which the answer is read out from an envelope as: "try to be nice to people, avoid eating fat, read a good book every now and then, get some walking in, and try to live together in peace and harmony with people of all creeds and nations."

No one agrees exactly on the meaning of life.

And that is great news for you!

Now you have a blank slate on which to discover YOUR purpose for YOUR life. It doesn't actually matter what the meaning is for "life, the universe and everything".

What is important is finding out YOUR purpose in life and then LIVING it.

Who This Book is For

So are you in the right place? If you are between 9 and 90 and nod your head at any of these statements, then you are in the perfect spot:

- You would love a simple, fast and robust method of finding your purpose.
- You are in a funk and want a quick way of refocusing your life on something more positive and meaningful.
- You haven't really thought about finding your purpose until now but sometimes do wonder about why you are here or what is life about.

Chapter Five invites you to find your purpose in 15 minutes, and I fully expect some eager readers to head straight there! I do suggest to get your mindset in order before launching into the 15-minute exercise and first read the next couple of chapters that explain why you have not found your purpose before now and then discover why it is mission critical to do so.

Once you find your purpose in 15 minutes you may be thinking "What now?" This book will show you how you can make your newfound purpose an integral part of your life—even if your current day-to-day looks nothing like it. It also gives suggestions on how to calibrate with your purpose when you go out of alignment and what to do with the naysayers who don't like the new purpose-driven you.

If you enjoyed the chance to reflect and dream and want to go further, there are some interesting and thought-provoking tests, questions and exercises so you can find out even more about how you tick and what is truly important to the real you. The book wraps up with a few suggestions to supercharge your new, purposeful life.

WHY I WROTE THIS BOOK

Other than the fact that it seems like one of the most significant things we as humans have the privilege of contemplating, why write a book on finding your purpose?

To be ridiculously honest with you, the first reason is because I am turning 42 this year. Yes, the favorite pop culture answer to the meaning of life created an impetus to write a book on purpose.

It also seemed like the next logical step after publishing a book on goal setting. The trouble was that in *Super Sexy Goal Setting*, I advised readers to skip over the step of finding their life purpose before setting goals as I thought it would take too much time and may even stop the more important task of goal setting completely.

I was also drawn towards writing a book on purpose as I was fortunate to attend Tony Robbins' Date with Destiny event earlier this year. During the six grueling but phenomenal days we did a lot of work on ourselves to discover who we truly are and what our ideal lives would look like if we erased our fears and limiting beliefs and reached for the stars. We ended the event writing a mission statement for our dream lives. Look, the event was amazing, BUT it took us six days to get to our purposes! Six days!

This is my key issue with finding your purpose and why I advised against it in *Super Sexy Goal Setting*. In all the research I did, finding your purpose always seemed to take hours of contemplating about your childhood, or your ideal life or what legacy you want to leave. Many guides I read on the topic wanted me to tap into my intuition and discover what my soul was telling me my life purpose was. Look, I love a bit of woo-woo, but when it comes to finding my life purpose, I didn't want to rely on my fickle and often absent intuition, my poor memory of my childhood wishes or my dismally unimaginative vision of a future me.

I loved every minute at Date with Destiny, but the whole experience provoked me to reconsider my belief that finding my purpose had to take ages. After the event, I asked myself a radical question: instead of a few days could someone be prompted to work out his or her purpose in a few minutes?

I wanted a simple, practical tool that could spell out a life purpose in a quick and easy way. I wanted to figure out what my life purpose was in the shortest amount of time and then get on with the more important job—living it.

And I wanted to help as many people as possible do this, too.

DEFINITIONS

Look, I am sorry, I hate to do this, but we all must get clear on the main terms in this area, otherwise things can get downright confusing.

Purpose of life: There are many definitions of purpose, so I have used a widely accepted understanding. Your life purpose is your WHY for being here. It is what you live for, what is important to you and what makes your life significant and worthwhile. This book will use 'purpose', 'your purpose', 'life purpose' or 'purpose of life' interchangeably.

Meaning of life: This is almost the same as 'purpose of life', although it seems to have a broader reach. People often ask what is the purpose of MY life and what is the meaning of life in general.

Destiny: The simple meaning of destiny is the things that will happen in the future including what you will do and the type of person you will be. 'Destiny' can sometimes imply that your future is decided by and controlled by a powerful and mysterious force.

Fate: Very similar to destiny, 'fate' can simply mean what happens to a person. It can also be extended to mean a power that controls events so they cannot be changed. It is often associated with an adverse outcome or death.

Dream: A dream is something amazing that you want to happen or you hope to achieve in the future but may be considered hard or unlikely.

Calling: A calling is a strong impulse to a course of action especially if there is a conviction it will be socially valuable. It is mostly connected with being attracted to a profession, career or work that helps others.

Vision: A vision is an idea or plan for the future. It is usually related to a specific organization or project.

Mission: An aim that is very important or a strong commitment to do or achieve something. Sometimes a purpose statement is called a mission statement.

Legacy: Something that has been achieved or exists after a person stops working or dies. Ultimately it is the thing for which you will be remembered.

In summary, purpose can also be interchanged with the words 'meaning', 'vision' and 'mission', and at a stretch it could be suggested with the words 'destiny', 'fate', 'calling' and 'legacy'.

No wonder no one tries to find his or her purpose! Just navigating the language around it is difficult enough. Never mind. Let's move on.

PARTS OF PURPOSE

Purpose is your big picture WHY, your highest reason for being here. To create a short, positive and powerful purpose statement, use this simple formula:

Your purpose is about who you want to BE and what you want to DO so that you have an IMPACT on others.

Your purpose statement is written using this template:

'The purpose of my life is to (be and/or do) _____ to (impact) _____'.

The BE and DO part is self-enhancing. It is the passions, strengths and values you have or aspire to embody. **Passions** are sometimes confused with purpose but are not the same. A passion is something you are strongly interested in, what you love to do, what you enjoy or what excites you. The root of the word comes from the Latin 'passio' meaning 'to suffer', so it implies you care so deeply that it hurts. If this seems a little too intense, then just think of what you like to do or what you are curious about. **Strengths** are talents or abilities that you have. Things that you are good at, that you would be able to teach to someone or qualities that give you an advantage or make you more effective. **Values** are what you care about, what matters most to you and what you stand for. Values are principles and emotional states that are important to you. There is a lot of overlap between these three areas.

The IMPACT part is self-transcending. This contribution aspect makes your purpose greater than a goal with its focus on your relationship to, sharing of your gifts with or impact on others (all others or a particular group).

Sources

Although this is merely one interpretation of what purpose is and one way to write out a purpose statement, it is based on a lot of research on this topic. Here are some of the main sources of how this purpose statement was developed:

- Positive psychology: describes a meaningful life as using your strengths in the service of something larger than you
- Bluezones: researchers who study the healthiest and longest living communities define purpose as a cross

section between what your values are, what you like to do, what you are good at and what you have to give

- Victor Frankl, a holocaust survivor who wrote the bestseller, *Man's Search for Meaning* saw three possible sources of meaning—work (doing something significant), love (caring for another) and in courage during difficult times
- Jack Canfield, author of *Success Principles,* states that "Ultimately our purpose is to serve each other with the expression of who we are in the world."
- In the book *The Top Five Regrets of the Dying*, overall what mattered most to the dying was how much happiness they brought to those they loved and how much time they spent doing things they loved
- Mike Sherbakov from The Greatness Foundation states that your purpose is the intersection of what you are passionate about, what you are good at and your connection to the world—what problems you want to fix
- In research, three factors stood out as predictors of happy 100-year-olds—the ability to get over disappointment, an outward view of life (caring about others and being involved positively in society) and a passion that is actively pursued

My Purpose Statement

Chapter Five provides the step-by-step instructions plus the top BE, DO and IMPACT words that can be slotted into the purpose template to help you easily write your ideal purpose statement in minutes.

Before that, dive a bit deeper into why you haven't tried to find your purpose in life up until now, get answers to some of the main questions you may have on finding your purpose, plus understand some of the benefits of a purpose-driven life.

At the end of each chapter you will be able to read some real life purpose statements generously supplied by a tribe of early volunteers of this 15-minute purpose exercise. Some statements are very short, some are long, some fit into this template strictly and some use it as a jumping off point to develop their perfect purpose. All are different and reflect the unique true self of the individual. I am full of deep gratitude to these life purpose guinea pigs. Thank you so much for your time and feedback.

To kick things off, here is my purpose statement:

> Julie: *The purpose of my life is to be my best self, full of love, energy and fun ('sparkle'), so I can continue to learn and create and then inspire others to achieve their potential.*

3

PURPOSE QUESTIONS (AND A WEE RANT)

 '*Life's but ... a tale told by an idiot, full of sound and fury, signifying nothing.*' – William Shakespeare's *Macbeth*, spoken by Macbeth

Objection Questions

Finding your life purpose can be confrontational. Here are some of the main objections to attempting to figure out a purpose in life in the form of questions:

> My life has been good without knowing my purpose, so why should I?
> What if I figure out my purpose and my life doesn't reflect it at all?
> What is the point of the 'find your life purpose' exercise again?
> What if I write out my purpose statement and it is not 'right'?

Do I really have to figure out the purpose of my life?

Won't it take up too much time to get an answer?

If I had a purpose, wouldn't I just know it?

Isn't it a lot of hard work, and for what?

Can my life purpose be changed?

Does everyone have a purpose?

Do I have to change my life?

What is the point of it all?

What IS the Point of it All?

The answers to these questions are in the next chapter. But why do we have so many objections to finding our purpose?

A lot of it stems from not being sure life has any meaning at all. If life has no meaning, then there seems to be zero point trying to extract out a purpose for our lives from our meaningless existence.

There is no real reason to think there is any purpose or meaning to our brief time here on Earth. We are merely an accident of time, space, and matter. We came to be through chaotic processes of physics and evolution, which is great for us, but essentially meaningless.

The universe is estimated to be about 91 billion light years in diameter. Think long and hard about that. Light travels at 186,000 miles per second. It takes eight minutes just for sunlight to reach Earth. Try and picture just how enormous 91 billion light years is. You can't.

We live on a little spinning planet in the middle of a solar system on the edge of a galaxy tucked into a corner of a vast universe. Imagine how trivial we are—our small galaxy, our tiny solar system, our miniscule planet. We could not be more insignificant in the greater scheme of things. In this gigantic swirling void of mostly nothingness, humans are but motes of stardust.

Many people seem to be just marking time—fidgeting between "the maternity ward and crematorium" as British philosopher, Alan Watts, aptly puts it. For most of us our day-to-day struggles to be a good person and to do well in the world will be forgotten and irrelevant in a period of mere months or years.

None of us is immortal. Each of us has maybe 100 years to make our mark, to do something with our lives. It doesn't seem like much time to create meaning. Death is inevitable yet terrifying, as despite our best efforts to believe in something beyond it, no one knows for sure. According to anthropologist and writer, Ernest Becker, this deep existential anxiety underlies everything we do, so any meaning we attempt our life to have is shaped by this innate desire to never die.

Hence many try to create a lasting legacy. You are one of around seven billion people currently alive, so how can anything you do truly matter? Very few of us will do anything in our lives that will have any importance beyond our own life spans and our own friends and families. A few people will do something that changes our world, but even Albert Einstein, Nelson Mandela and Beyoncé will eventually be forgotten. These children we work so hard to raise are going to die, too, as will their children and so on. What is the point of making an impact, anyway? Trying to do so feels at worst fruitless and, at best, like littering.

It is a tendency of humankind to think that we must somehow be very important because we have sentience and civilization (such as it is) and symphony orchestras and great art and the Internet and whatnot, and it seems too amazing to have occurred by chance. But we are just bags of skin with trillions of bugs inside of us. Bugs similar to the type that will be on the planet long after the zombie apocalypse wipes us all out and we are all gone.

When even our briefest of time here on Earth is ridiculous, absurd and nonsensical, how can we extract any kind of purpose from it? How can a 15-second video of a rat transporting a slice of pizza down some stairs get over 8.5 million views, while human slavery be a bigger problem than it was 150 years ago? How can it be possible to order a burger via emojis, but there not be safe, clean drinking water available for everyone? What sort of world do we live in where news coverage centers on the Kardashian clan and the silly names they have given their children rather than the fact that topsoil and tigers are disappearing and the oceans are filling up with titanic amounts of plastic waste?

Life doesn't owe you anything. The universe does not care about you. The universe is mostly a freezing void. Eventually the sun will expand and swallow our planet and we will become extinct. Even if we have mastered interstellar travel (unlikely) the universe will eventually collapse upon itself. Nothing lasts.

To sum up: The universe is big and we are small. When you look at the size of universe and the expanse of time, nothing we ever do in our lives has any point at all.

Any way we look at it, life is insignificant, meaningless and absurd.

And a good day to you, sir.

Sunset Prescription

Wowsers, where did that all come from?

You are one tough, nihilistic-tasting cookie!

I prescribe taking a few deep breaths plus a mandatory viewing of the nearest sunset, stat!

In the next chapter we will address the objection questions and tell you why you absolutely NEED a purpose.

PURPOSE STATEMENTS

Carrie: *The purpose of my life is to be kind, positive and enjoy so that I can be brave, learn to teach and make a difference to my community.*

Ton: *To be a safe haven in order to ease suffering of all sentient beings.*

Lisa: *The purpose of my life is to be joyful and energetic, to be confident and always growing so I can inspire and empower others to create a life they love.*

Julia: *The purpose of my life is to grow! To grow in knowledge but also to grow food to feed people and contribute and to grow a peaceful garden farm and environment to better people, animals and nature.*

4

PURPOSE ANSWERS

> 'This is the true joy in life, being used for a purpose recognized by yourself as a mighty one. Being a force of nature instead of a feverish, selfish little clod of ailments and grievances, complaining that the world will not devote itself to making you happy.' – George Bernard Shaw

OBJECTION ANSWERS

Is there any way to overcome the notion that all life is meaningless? The answers to the main objections will help you to see another perspective and lead you to being excited about finding your purpose in the next chapter.

MY LIFE HAS BEEN GOOD WITHOUT KNOWING MY PURPOSE, SO WHY should I?

Worried you may upset the apple cart of your perfectly acceptable life? But you wouldn't be here if you weren't a little curious about how brilliant your life could be. After all, no matter how great our lives are, there is another level—one of passion, beauty, connection, energy and happiness.

I said it in *Super Sexy Goal Setting* and I will say it again: you owe it to the world to use up every single tiny ounce of all the resources and riches with which you were so fortunately bestowed to reach your potential, create value and share your gifts with the world. It would be a travesty if you just settled because you thought you didn't deserve even more from life.

WHAT IF I FIGURE OUT MY PURPOSE AND MY LIFE DOESN'T REFLECT it at all?

People find it intimidating to think about finding their purpose as it is very clear whether they are living it. Your purpose is a filter that you now can't ignore.

Don't worry if you find your purpose and your life looks nothing like it! You certainly don't have to ditch your current life. Knowing your purpose will give you some clarity around what you want and why you want it. It will help you say 'yes' to things that support it, and easily—and in a guilt-free way—say 'no' to things that have no place in your purpose-aligned life. Some people will find that their lives slowly ease into line with their purpose without a lot of effort. Others may make some drastic changes.

We will address this later, so please don't make it an excuse not to find your purpose at all. You can still find your purpose and start to use it as a guiding light, something to aspire to. And what if your life already DOES reflect your purpose?

Wouldn't it be nice to know with certainty that you are already living your ideal life?

WHAT IS THE POINT OF THE 'FIND YOUR LIFE PURPOSE' EXERCISE **again?**

Our entire lives are about creating meaning from what happens around us, so why not create a big picture vision that, well, means something to you? Isn't it a good idea to tap into what your life is really about instead of defaulting to any old meaning?

At the very least, the 15-minute purpose exercise will give you an insight into YOU. Taking a step back and tapping into what you like to do, what you are good at and what is important to you often brings out the best in people. It will show you where you can combine your passions, strengths and core values to shine in the world.

And don't worry; you really don't have to figure out something special or amazing. The template will direct you to create a purpose statement that is about being your best self and being nice to others. That is all.

What WOULD be special is if more people started living their lives in this way.

WHAT IF I WRITE OUT MY PURPOSE STATEMENT AND IT IS NOT 'right'?

It doesn't have to be perfect. What you come up with is better than the nothing you had before, true?

DO I REALLY **HAVE** TO FIGURE OUT THE PURPOSE OF MY LIFE?

No. You don't HAVE to find your purpose. As my coach says, the only thing you HAVE to do in life is breathe. Sit with that for a moment. You also don't have to watch a sunset, walk in a forest, eat chocolate, visit a museum or smell the roses. But it adds a richness and depth to your life that makes it worth living, so why wouldn't you? What have you got to lose? Especially if it only takes a few minutes.

Won't it take up too much time to get an answer?

No. Only 15 minutes. It's in the title of the book.

If I had a purpose wouldn't I just know it?

I am a pragmatic kind of girl and I like the thought of deciding on a purpose and directing my future, BUT I am also a romantic and I like the thought that life is magical and the universe may just have a plan for me. So which is it? Let's examine the arguments.

In the blue corner we have author and wise soul, Martha Beck, amongst others. They say that every human being has a divine purpose in life, a mission to fulfill, a path to follow. Our right lives whisper at us from our deepest selves. You may think you have no idea, but your soul knows why you are here. During idle times, when you dream or if you really lean into your intuition and listen, your true self tells you what your direction should be and what your destiny is.

Many people understand this at some level as they feel something is missing, that they are not fulfilling their destiny or contributing to the world in a way they know they can. Often it is because our daily lives cloud our 'North Star'—Martha's metaphor for our life purpose—and we need to find ways to make the night sky clear once again.

You are not 'deciding' on a purpose, but instead unearthing or rediscovering it. You already have it but want to bring it out into the open and in doing so become more of your essential core self: more YOU.

BUT—having to dig deep and uncover your perfect life purpose meant only for you—well, I hate to say it, but this is an awful lot of pressure. Also this seems to link into a notion of pre-destiny, which makes me feel a bit icky, like I don't have the freedom to choose. And it implies you have only one unchangeable purpose whereas I like to think you can find a general purpose and tweak it a bit as you progress through your life.

So what is the alternative?

In the red corner we have educator and chess master, Adam Robinson, amongst others. This is their point of view: you can simply decide on the type of person you want to become and how you want to live your life. Decide on it and then live it.

Your future is not pre-destined. It is based on what you are doing and thinking right now and so can be shaped. There is a choice in every moment. Take charge of your life and your future by taking charge of your present.

Stop searching for your purpose. Stop wasting time looking. Invent it. Find something meaningful and important to you and direct your life so you nurture it. Also know that you may not have one true calling, but a multitude of purposes as you grow and evolve to create an overall excellent life.

BUT—if you don't have an innate purpose or if you have many of them is it really a true mission? If it is not, then what is the point of finding it? This way at best seems not very magical and at worst seems a bit 'fake it till you make it' in style.

JULIE SCHOOLER

So, does it really matter? Whether you discover OR decide on your purpose may just be a difference in semantics. I have found 'find' sits relatively nicely in the middle of the two ways of looking at purpose. You may see the use of 'discover', 'uncover', 'create' or 'decide' instead of 'find'. It doesn't infer I agree with one viewpoint over the other.

Most people are happy to sit at the debate table rather than take the leap to find their purpose, as then they may have to get honest with themselves, vulnerable, and uncomfortable. They would rather argue all day long than take action on a purpose-driven life.

Either way, your dreams will remain dreams unless you find courage to achieve them. Divine inspiration is unlikely to smack you over the head, but regardless of what you believe, you are designed with the ability to determine the life you are meant to live.

Whether we already have a purpose deep inside of all of us, or we create it with our drive and action is beside the point. If you can't elucidate it, don't have it clearly in mind, then it is not helpful to you.

You want your purpose to be front and center, not whispering at you from the sidelines.

Isn't it a lot of hard work, and for what?

First, I hope you can see by now that finding your purpose doesn't have to be hard work. So to answer the 'for what' piece—here are some benefits of knowing your purpose.

Personal development master, Tony Robbins, has popularized the theory that we all have six human needs. These are needs, not wants. We crave these on a deep level. One of the primary needs is a need for **certainty**—to feel safe and secure and to know that our expectations will be met.

Figuring out your purpose meets your need for certainty in a major way. It can simplify and clarify your life. It is a filter for action. A lighthouse that provides direction. It is a foundation to structure your life around. It assists with prioritizing your time around what is really important to you.

In tough times, purpose can give you an inner drive to continue. When times are easier it brings more energy and compassion into your life. In the research—check out the Bluezones website—it is linked to a longer, happier life, which is statistically significant at a whopping seven years longer!

Other studies have linked knowing your purpose with better physical health (e.g.: better immunity, less likelihood of dementia), improved mental health (e.g.: lower rates of depression) and superior overall wellbeing (e.g.: better sleep, more friends).

According to big Tony, we have six needs, but only four of them—certainty, variety, significance and love—are met in everyone. The other two needs for growth and contribution are not always considered. Finding your purpose is a way to meet these two essential but sometimes neglected needs.

Purpose helps you to grow as it illuminates where you must move to in order to be your best self. This may be challenging, but ultimately any growth helps you to feel fulfilled.

Even more important, a purpose is not fully realized unless it has a transcendent part to it, a view on impacting, sharing or giving to others. When you are doing what you are meant to do, you benefit the world in an irreplaceable way. If you do not share your unique gifts and potentially help others, then you are doing a disservice to the world. In short, finding your purpose assists you in meeting your very real need for contribution.

How you can use your new purpose to meet your essential needs for growth and contribution is discussed in the 'Supercharge Your Purpose' chapter.

CAN MY LIFE PURPOSE BE CHANGED?

Figuring out your purpose can be a once in a lifetime thing, or you can reflect on it each year or two and refine or tweak it. It should help you feel focused, not confined. You never do anything for your whole life, so why would your purpose be any different?

DOES EVERYONE HAVE A PURPOSE?

I think so, but it doesn't really matter what I think. What do you think? And do you really care? Isn't it more important to decide on your own purpose?

DO I HAVE TO CHANGE MY LIFE?

People get scared of change. But who you really are deep down is not changing. You are aligning more with your essential self. Some of your patterns and behaviors may change. How the external world reacts is what you are really worried about. We will talk in depth about how to deal with this later. But for now, get excited. After all, change is inevitable, the only constant in life is change, and now YOU are driving it.

. . .

WHAT IS THE POINT OF IT ALL?

It is easy to feel overwhelmed and insignificant. But the very fact that we live in a vast universe filled with mostly nothing and we are alive, here, right now is a miracle beyond miracles that is mind-bogglingly amazing.

> Don't think of the universe as nothingness. Think of it as limitless.

Sure, everyone dies, the end can come at any moment and death seems like a terrible and permanent conclusion. But death is what makes life profound. Our limited time here IS what is meaningful. Imagine how bored immortals like vampires would be!

Let's enjoy the journey instead of riding out the time until it is all over. We owe the gift of life our appreciation and action, not our disdain and lethargy. As cosmologist, Lawrence Krauss notes, even if the universe doesn't have a purpose, "We should not despair, but humbly rejoice in... our brief moment in the sun."

All of us have no idea what we are doing here on a fast spinning planet in the corner of a small galaxy on the edge of a vast universe, so we may as well play in the nonsense and absurdity and try to have a blast. Don't fight it. Live in the ridiculous.

We are currently alive in the most safe and abundant time in human history, on a planet thriving with life, with a sun that shines, fresh water that pours out of the sky, and sometimes when the combination of the two is just right, we get rainbows. As Jen Sincero says in her fabulous book, *You are a Badass*: "The fact that we aren't stumbling around in a state of awe is appalling."

We have now smashed through your main objections to finding your purpose, and you should be absolutely pumped and ready to find your purpose in 15 minutes in the next chapter.

PURPOSE STATEMENTS

Grace: *The purpose of my life is to be fulfilled, healthy, and fun, so that I can share my sincere and grateful self with the world.*

Vartika: *The purpose of my life is to be happy, to have fun, and to contribute to the community as well as to inspire others.*

Jackie: *The purpose of my life is to be living, happy, healthy, fun, to grow and be compassionate to make a difference and gift to others.*

Catherine: *The purpose of my life is to solve challenging health problems to enable people to move forward with their lives.*

FIND YOUR PURPOSE IN 15 MINUTES

 'Every day, think as you wake up, today I am fortunate to be alive, I have a precious human life, I am not going to waste it.' – Dalai Lama

ONE LAST OBJECTION

You may be thinking "How can this be my real purpose if it doesn't take a lot of time and work?" The fact that it takes 15 minutes doesn't make it any less real. Plucking the words from a list doesn't make it any less relevant. And using a template as a kind of 'paint by numbers' purpose statement doesn't make it any less original or unique to you.

One of the early volunteers said:

> "I really loved this! I was shocked to have broken my perception that finding my purpose had to be difficult and time consuming – thank you!"

Purpose Recap

Your purpose is your WHY for being here. It is what you live for, what is important to you and what makes your life significant and worthwhile. Don't worry if you find your purpose and your life looks nothing like it! You can start to use it as a guiding light, something to aspire to.

A purpose statement should be short, positive and powerfully resonate with you.

The template below is a useful foundation that can also be rearranged to fit your unique purpose statement.

> **Definition:** Your purpose is about who you want to BE and what you want to DO so that you have an IMPACT on others.

> **Template:** 'The purpose of my life is to (be and/or do) _____ to (impact) _____.'

Purpose Examples

E.g.: The purpose of my life is to be courageous, abundance-oriented and full of gratitude so that I can share my gifts with others and help the environment.

E.g.: The purpose of my life is to be loving, joyful and healthy so that I can learn, grow and create and then encourage others to success.

E.g.: The purpose of my life is to be full of passion so I can use my determination and inquisitive nature to help to make a difference in my community and the world.

THE FAB LIST

One of the most difficult parts of finding your purpose is coming up with the right words to use. Here is where the 15-minute purpose exercise makes things super easy for you.

It gives you all the words you need!

It simply hands them out on a silver platter.

First is '**The Fab List**' – a selection of 20 positive words along with their associated words and short phrases. Simply look over these 100+ tasty bites and choose your favorites to use in the your 'BE' and 'DO' elements in the first part of the purpose statement.

- Love – nice, kind, caring, grace
- Healthy – energy, vitality, wellbeing, fit, strong
- Happy – joy, cheerful, positive, optimistic, fulfilled
- Fun – enjoy, playful, humor, laughter
- Grow – learn, discover, improve, master, knowledge
- Achieve – accomplish, success, excellence, live my dreams
- Create – imagine, innovate, invent, art
- Courage – brave, confident, bold, adventurous, face fear
- Passionate – excitement, enthusiastic, zest for life
- Give – help, contribute, serve, generous, benevolent
- Peace – calm, simplicity, tranquil, serene, rest
- Curious – inquisitive, interested, wonder, be in awe
- Spiritual – aware, conscious, wholeness, mindful, transcendent
- Integrity – fair, honest, sincere, true, open

- Authentic – real, genuine, be me, be myself, be true to me
- Ideal self – be my best self, reach my potential, be a good person
- Appreciate – gratitude, grateful, thankful, treasure
- Compassionate – supportive, considerate, empathetic, thoughtful, warm
- Persistent – determined, driven, motivated, ambitious, grit
- Abundance – wealth, freedom, beauty, wisdom, power

The Impact Lists

The two '**Impact Lists**' are then used to complete the second half of the purpose statement about your impact on others. There are verbs such as 'give', 'work towards' and 'inspire' and then nouns such as 'others', 'my community' and 'the world' to select from.

Verbs

- Give – help, gift, provide, give abundance to
- Share – serve, share my gifts, contribute, nourish, delight
- Connect – teach, write, speak, learn, read
- Lead – empower, inspire, encourage, spread magic, focus on
- Accept – listen, understand, heal, forgive
- Make a difference – give hope to, work towards, stand for, challenge

Nouns

- Non-specific – others, humans, all beings, people, creatures
- Specific – organizations, causes, charities, community, groups
- Friends and Family – loved ones, my family, my children, my tribe
- General – the world, the environment, nature, my legacy

Word Lists Housekeeping

Use any of the words. They are displayed in a manner that is meant to make them easier to read and choose, not because the 'main' word is more important than the associated words and phrases.

Feel free to highlight all the words you like. Then try and narrow down to the most important ones for you. It is okay to drop a few of the words when writing out your purpose statement. They won't mind.

You may need to change the words slightly to fit into your purpose statement ('love' to 'loving', 'create' to 'creative', 'power' to 'powerful', etc.).

If you have a word not in the lists that best suits your purpose, please use it. People say these lists nudge them to come up with other words, or they add a faith-based component as well.

Find Your Purpose in 15 Minutes Instructions

1. Take a deep breath and say in an excited voice: 'I will find my purpose today!'

2. Keep this purpose statement template in mind:

'The purpose of my life is to (be and/or do) _____ to (impact) _____'

3. Read **The Fab List** below and highlight or write down any words that resonate the most with you. Most people eventually settle on between 2 and 8 words:

- Love – nice, kind, caring, grace
- Healthy – energy, vitality, wellbeing, fit, strong
- Happy – joy, cheerful, positive, optimistic, fulfilled
- Fun – enjoy, playful, humor, laughter
- Grow – learn, discover, improve, master, knowledge
- Achieve – accomplish, success, excellence, live my dreams
- Create – imagine, innovate, invent, art
- Courage – brave, confident, bold, adventurous, face fear
- Passionate – excitement, enthusiastic, zest for life
- Give – help, contribute, serve, generous, benevolent
- Peace – calm, simplicity, tranquil, serene, rest
- Curious – inquisitive, interested, wonder, be in awe
- Spiritual – aware, conscious, wholeness, mindful, transcendent
- Integrity – fair, honest, sincere, true, open
- Authentic – real, genuine, be me, be myself, be true to me
- Ideal self – be my best self, reach my potential, be a good person
- Appreciate – gratitude, grateful, thankful, treasure
- Compassionate – supportive, considerate, empathetic, thoughtful, warm
- Persistent – determined, driven, motivated, ambitious, grit
- Abundance – wealth, freedom, beauty, wisdom, power

4. Read the **Impact Lists** below and highlight or write down the verbs and nouns that fit the impact part of your purpose statement. Most people choose between 1 and 3 words from each list:

Verbs

- Give – help, gift, provide, give abundance to
- Share – serve, share my gifts, contribute, nourish, delight
- Connect – teach, write, speak, learn, read
- Lead – empower, inspire, encourage, spread magic, focus on
- Accept – listen, understand, heal, forgive
- Make a difference – give hope to, work towards, stand for, challenge

Nouns

- Non-specific – others, humans, all beings, people, creatures
- Specific – organizations, causes, charities, community, groups
- Friends and Family – loved ones, my family, my children, my tribe
- General – the world, the environment, nature, my legacy

5. Take out a pen and paper and write out

'The purpose of my life is to ____'

6. Add your favorite words from **The Fab List** and the **Impact Lists** into the template and rewrite your purpose statement until it powerfully resonates with you. This may take a handful of attempts but you WILL get there.

7. Read your final purpose statement aloud.

Congratulations, just like that you have found your purpose!

Is it Good Enough?

You have a purpose statement but you are not sure if it is 'good enough'. Use this quick checklist to find out:

A purpose statement should be:

- short (one or two sentences)
- positive (makes you very happy)
- easy to experience (every single day)
- powerfully resonate with you (just feels right)

If you are not sure if it is quite right yet, put it aside for today, look at it with fresh eyes tomorrow and tweak it if needed.

Maybe you still think your purpose statement is not 'good enough' as it was such a quick and simple exercise. This is what some of the early volunteers had to say:

> "I hadn't ever thought to do this in writing before, but this made it so easy; it's focused my mind and heart and I'm glad to see that my purpose statement is actually true to my life now and shows so much growth potential."

> "This is very insightful and I wish I had done it a long time ago. It's comforting and liberating at the same time. It makes all the noise fall away and gives that clarity we are always looking to find."

> "Thank you for giving me some of my drive back that I have been struggling with."

"I love my purpose statement. It really resonates with me and I use it every day. Thank you."

PLEASE, if you haven't done the 15-minute purpose exercise yet, give it a go.

Wear It In

Your purpose statement may feel a little tight, a bit scratchy. The next chapter explains how to ingrain your purpose statement so it becomes comfortably part of you. The following chapter gives you some tips on how to really live your purpose, even if your life looks nothing like your purpose statement.

Stick around.

Finding your purpose in 15 minutes is just the beginning.

Purpose Statements

Jodi: *The purpose of my life is to be authentic and to live my truth so others will be inspired to do the same.*

Cill: *The purpose of my life is to encourage bravery and compassion by being courageous and caring to all the people I am in contact with.*

Nicole: *The purpose of my life is to create and nourish loving relationships so that I can live a life full of love and fulfillment and hopefully inspire others to do the same and succeed in their world.*

Georgie: *The purpose of my life is to be conscious in reaching my full potential through living a life full of love, happiness, compassion, joy, knowledge, abundance and gratitude by being open and mastering my true self; so that I can be creative, teach, empower, inspire, help and heal others and the earth by sharing my love, wisdom and gifts.*

6

PLANT YOUR PURPOSE IN YOUR MIND, HEART AND SOUL

 'Life is either a daring adventure or nothing at all.' – Helen Keller

CROSS IT OFF THE LIST

Wow, just like that you have your purpose statement! You have a simple way to think about and express your life purpose. You can check 'find the purpose of your life' off your to-do list!

So what do you do now?

There are three simple steps that will take you from finding your purpose to thoroughly enfolding it into your life. The steps are:

1. Read, display and review your purpose so it is ingrained in your mind
2. Link practices around it such as incantations, visualizations, empowering questions or a gratitude ritual so it is embedded in your heart

3. Find ways to use it as a filter and a guide every day in the real world so it is part of the core YOU, in your soul

Let's go over each of these steps in more detail...

1. PLANT YOUR PURPOSE IN YOUR MIND

Make sure that you have your purpose statement somewhere you have easy access to it and see it every day. Use a pen and paper version or print it out and stick it to your wall, on the fridge or on the bathroom mirror. For those who are more private, put it inside the door to your wardrobe or tuck it into a journal you write in regularly.

If you have an electronic document of your purpose, place that document on your computer desktop, or add it into your notes app or books app on your phone so you can open it up and read it regularly.

Some of you may want to share your newfound purpose on your favorite social media feed, on Pinterest or on your own blog. Sharing it with others keeps you accountable to live your life on purpose, but it does have a potential downside in that some people may be less than enthusiastic about it.

A fun and completely optional way to display your purpose statement is to create a 'vision board' of it. A vision board is any sort of board on which you display images that represent items that can relate to your purpose—images of role models you want to be like, what you want to do and create in your lifetime and who you want to help or share your gifts with. Create one the old-fashioned way out of cutouts from magazines stuck to a big piece of paper or cardboard. Or combine some pictures into an online board on Pinterest or elsewhere.

An extra cool idea is to take a photo of your written purpose statement or its physical vision board and upload it so it becomes your computer screen saver or wallpaper on your phone. We look at our phones on average over 100 times a day (yes really!), so your purpose statement will be reviewed, at least subconsciously, an enormous amount.

These ideas help you remember and easily recite your purpose statement. At this point I usually get asked what to do if you want to change your purpose. If it seems fine to you, then please don't amend it unless it is a tweak as a result of the extra introspection (navel-gazing) chapters coming up next. Leave it for at least six months, and then use the tools above to read and remember a revised version after that point.

2. PLANT YOUR PURPOSE IN YOUR HEART

Displaying and reading your purpose statement on a repeated basis gives you a cognitive level of understanding it. You will know your purpose inside out and back to front. But for it to really stick, you need to feel like it is part of you. It needs to connect with your emotional center, your heart.

There are a number of ways to do this, so select one or two and try them out. Some of them can also be mixed together to make a mega-tool. Yes, they may seem a bit strange, but they are also a bit of fun, so why not give them a go?

AFFIRMATIONS AND INCANTATIONS

Affirmations and incantations are long words that basically mean saying your purpose statement (or anything else) aloud, often and in a repeated fashion. Affirmations are associated with saying things in the mirror. Incantations are not usually in front of a mirror but have more power and emotion behind them. They are often done standing in a strong posture and speaking with a loud, confident voice. You can feel a little silly about it, but they are a great, no-cost way of embedding in your purpose statement. Plus they don't have to take up any extra time—do them while putting on your makeup or shaving, driving in your car or as part of your morning exercise and mindset routine.

EMPOWERING QUESTIONS

If you don't feel like you are quite up to affirmations and incantations, what can you do instead? Well just like the start of this paragraph, you can use questions in a more effective way. Using empowering questions has been found to have a greater impact on outcomes than affirmations because if a question is asked, even if it is not spoken aloud, your mind is still compelled to answer it. So ask yourself (silently or out loud) questions such as:

'How can I live my purpose even more?', or
'What is one thing I can do today to help me be more on purpose?' or
'What would the person I want to become do right now?'

Then listen to your heart's response.

VISUALIZATION

For the visual people or dreamers out there, there is a less noisy way of connecting deeply with your purpose. Take a few moments of alone time, get comfortable, close your eyes and imagine what your life would be like with your purpose fully realized. Create the most vivid and descriptive mental picture as you can. Invoke your senses: what would you be doing, seeing, smelling, feeling? Please try not to think about the 'how' of what you have just conjured up. Simply bask in the warm glow of your purpose-fuelled life visualization for a few moments.

Gratitude Ritual

Being grateful creates awareness of the good in your life. Gratitude studies have shown that an appreciation practice is associated with being more enthusiastic about life, being interested in the community, being kinder to others and getting better sleep, among a myriad of other positive outcomes. Be thankful for knowing you can easily find your purpose. Feel appreciative when you think of living your life on purpose. And feel gratitude in combination with any of the above techniques. It works especially well as part of the visualization exercise.

3. Plant Your Purpose in Your Soul

You may now be thinking that all this reciting of my purpose sounds great, BUT my life looks NOTHING like the purpose I wrote down! For some people this will be exciting and for others this will be downright scary. Now that you know your purpose there is no denying or ignoring it any longer, and this can be a challenging place to be.

The next chapter will go into more depth on how to live with purpose including tackling some of the major issues that can come up when you start to live with a mission in life. It will give you some tips on what to do to change your life so it starts to fit around your newfound purpose, how to get back in alignment when you derail from your purpose and what to do about the naysayers.

For now, here is the BEST tip to start living your life with your purpose front and center. Are you ready? Drum roll please…

SAY 'NO'.

Your purpose will mean some things need to be shed from your life. You need to remove the good to make way for the great. Putting boundaries around your purposeful life will feel right but will be difficult, at least at first. If you do not learn to say 'no', then you are saying 'YES' to someone else's agenda and 'NO' to yourself.

You can still be a lovely person and say no. Author, researcher and TED speaker, Brené Brown says: "Compassionate people ask for what they need. They say no when they need to, and when they say yes, they mean it. They're compassionate because their boundaries keep them out of resentment."

Even in the nicest way possible, saying 'no' is uncomfortable, so practice on small things and build up. Here are a few ways to say 'no' politely:

- "Sounds wonderful, but that is not part of my work focus right now."
- "Sorry but my current commitments mean I cannot take that on."
- "It sounds amazing but I wouldn't be able to give that the attention it deserves."
- "I can't help you right now but I can schedule it after X date."

- "Sorry it is not my policy to do X." (People respect policies, even ones you have made up yourself!)

If a 'no' is done well, people should be happy with how clear you are and how committed you are to what is important to you. And if they are not happy? Well, their response is their problem. We will talk more about dealing with the critics in the next chapter.

KEEP CLIMBING

It may sound too easy to be true, but repeating your newfound purpose over and over WILL mean that you start to truly believe and embody your purpose. But we can't just live inside our heads and our hearts. We must start manifesting what our purpose is directing us to do.

Finding your purpose is your first stage. Believing it is the second. Living it is the third. Take it one rung at a time but keep moving up.

PURPOSE STATEMENTS

Nikita: *The purpose of my life is to be happy and peaceful so that I can connect and share delight with loved ones and the world.*

Sally: *The purpose of my life is to be constantly learning and writing so that I can help women everywhere share their unique gifts and create a life they love.*

Carole: *The purpose of my life is to be a good person, kind, successful, compassionate and living honestly and with integrity so that I can give generously, abundantly and with love to my tribe and to causes I believe in.*

Richard: *The purpose of my life is to be empathetic, to be curious to learn and challenge myself and create, to enable me to be content, supportive to people I care about, to have patience with myself and family and be there for my son as he grows.*

7

PURPOSE IN THE REAL WORLD

 'And the day came when the risk to remain tight in a bud was more painful than the risk it took to blossom.' – Anais Nin

THE 'N' ISSUES

You now have a purpose and you are trying hard to get it ingrained in your mind, heart and soul with the techniques from the last chapter, but you still might not be so sure exactly how to really LIVE it.

People who find their purpose end up in a few different categories. This chapter addresses your burning questions depending on where you have landed with your purpose.

Here are three main issues to acquiring a new purpose:

- The Non-believers: "I have found a purpose, but my life looks nothing like it. I don't truly believe I can live it, and I am not sure where to even begin."
- The Neglecters: "I have found a purpose, and it mostly matches my life already, so I am thrilled, but I can fall out of alignment with it and am not sure how to get back on track."
- The Naysayers: "I have found a purpose, I love it and I am embarking on making a few changes in my life, but now I am experiencing some negative reactions from other people."

HELP FOR THE NON-BELIEVERS

You have glimpsed your ultimate purpose, and now your mind is telling you that it is not possible to have a life that embraces it. This is a common but cruel reaction to finding your purpose. I understand wanting to hide from it. There is a lot of fear associated with purpose—fear of success, fear of failure, fear of what others may think.

Congratulations! Give yourself a pat on the back as you have overcome some of your fear to find your purpose. Most people don't even get that far. Now you have to fight your mind gremlins to really believe in it and start living it.

With curiosity and not judgment, look at the negative beliefs and limiting stories that your mind is telling you. Uncover what is behind you not allowing yourself to live your best life. Your thoughts are only thoughts; they are not necessarily true. What would happen if you just stopped believing that notion and started believed something that permitted you to live a life of purpose?

There is a ton more that can be said here, but please don't let some old story you have told yourself stop you from living the life you are supposed to live. Check out my book, *Crappy to Happy*, if all this piques your interest.

What do you do if you want to change your life but don't know where to start? Start doing something. Anything at all. You have now tapped into some of your passions, strengths and values. Take action on one of them. Choose an activity, hobby, side-hustle idea or problem in the world you would like to fix and start working on it. Take a class, find a mentor, join a team, create something. Start small and see where it leads. And if it doesn't work, try something else. Fail forward.

People think belief has to come before action, but often you can direct your behavior towards something and that changes your thinking about it. You are not going to be good at writing / dancing / engineering overnight, but by learning and practicing you develop these into strengths and passions that confirm your purpose. Clarity comes from taking action.

As blogger and potty mouth, Mark Mansen states: "Life is about not knowing and then doing something anyway. All of life is like this. It never changes."

Purpose is only a concept until you pick a direction and start to learn and master some skills. You can't share your gifts with the world until you have put some genuine effort into trying things that you think you may enjoy and want to share. Think of it as growing into your purpose. Everyone knows growing up does not happen overnight.

HELP FOR THE NEGLECTERS

You found your purpose earlier and realized that you have been living it all along. Your purpose statement fits like a glove over your existing life. You feel like you are already mostly living your purpose. Congratulations, you are one lucky human.

The main issue you may have is sometimes forgetting about or neglecting your purpose. You stray off the track of your purpose-driven life and need to be guided back. First, don't beat yourself up as no one lives his or her life entirely on purpose all the time. Be kind to yourself. You have permission to not write the next book or build your socially conscious business and instead scroll, binge watch or get to the next game level.

Simply remember to check in now and again between the different areas of your life—relationships, work, health etc.—and see if you are mostly living your purpose.

If you fall out of alignment, pull yourself back in with grace and without judgment.

What you can do to align with your purpose doesn't have to be extraordinary. Spend time with your kids without your phone, pay someone a compliment or give yourself an hour to go for a run, read a book or paint a picture. Reread your purpose statement, do exercises like incantations to get your purpose ingrained, and wake up to a new day with your purpose woven even more into the fabric of your life.

Dealing with the Naysayers

The two above issues are mostly within your control to solve. You decide what to believe, how to take action and when to pull your life back in line with your purpose.

What can you do if something is outside your immediate control? What do you do if you have a negative reaction from others?

First, check whether there really is an undesirable, external response to you living your purpose. Often people have a mindset that everybody won't like the new you or that 'people' will be upset if you change your life. Most of this is just garbage spewing out from your mind gremlins and does not reflect your reality. If there is no actual discouraging reaction but you still think there is, then you need to do some work on your limiting beliefs— question them and cut them out if they don't serve you.

Second, you can change your life subtly. Move incrementally towards your purpose. You don't have to tell anyone. You can decide to be more cheerful at home, write a book on the train to work or save a few dollars each week to visit that place in the world you have always dreamed of seeing. Honestly, most people won't notice. You will have a lighter feeling and you will know you have put in the work to create it, but others, even close loved ones, will continue on like normal.

Last, yes, sometimes, there is an actual proper attack on the new you, which, remember, is really the core you. Occasionally naysayers try to sabotage you working towards your purpose. First, unless they are close to you, don't pay them any notice. So what if the media or the culture doesn't like it? But if they are connected to you in some way—family, close friends, colleagues —then you may have to deal with it.

If there is a comment or even friction from your family, explain that you are working on becoming nicer and happier for them. Shift the focus back to them. Tell them you are going to be the same person but more YOU: less distracted, less stressed, happier and more fun. How could anyone say they wouldn't like that? Plus they are your family; they should want the best for you. If friends or colleagues are questioning you, then use this tool from author and wise soul, Martha Beck: practice saying this simple phrase to any naysayer:

"All is well."

If there is still some conflict, realize that their reactions are just coming from their own needs, and you have the power to respond in the most resourceful way you can. Repeat that this is how things will be, be gracious when interacting with them and limit your time with the naysayers to what is absolutely necessary. Then go and find a tribe that understands and respects your new, beautiful, authentic way of living. They are out there waiting for you.

LIVING ON PURPOSE

You have taken steps to make your life match your purpose, but how do you really know you are living it? It may feel good, but it may not. New challenges arise and sometimes life can seem harder than it once was. You could take that as a sign that you are not living your real purpose or living it in the right way.

Many people say they notice that even though there will be issues and stumbles, overall they feel more energized, confident and free. How do you feel in general now that you have defined your purpose?

I know my purpose is shining through when there is some unexpected benefit or strange coincidence that arises from my new way of living. Since becoming an author, through a series of small-world connections, I managed to get back in touch with a friend with whom I lost contact with over ten years ago. I was also gifted a crystal bracelet from another friend who credits me with partly inspiring her to start her own side business. These are not outcomes I could have possibly directed or foreseen, but these ripple effects make me feel like my purpose-driven life is on the right track.

Now that your purpose is clear to you, your life WILL change. This is a scary concept—no one loves change—but you can navigate this with acceptance and grace. So whether you decide to take a big leap or let your newfound purpose guide you into incremental shifts, welcome to your new life.

Navel-gazing

Many of the early volunteers for the find your purpose in 15-minute exercise loved being given the chance for a bit of introspection and reflection. There were comments like:

> "I liked how it made me reflect on my life, loved it, thank you."

> "I can feel confident that I've reviewed all areas of my life, my priorities and my inner desires."

> "This reflection was a great start to my day!"

> "It pushed me out of my comfort zone. As a typical man this makes you think about feelings and what you want from life which does get a little bit deep for a Tuesday lunchtime but it's always good to check your direction."

The next three chapters are for those of you, like these early volunteers, who really enjoyed the short exercise in finding your purpose and want some more of that juicy goodness.

- Chapter Eight suggests personality and psychological tests you can take to find out more about yourself.
- Chapter Nine gives a variety of questions to ponder.
- Chapter Ten provides some exercises that give you a deeper grasp of who you are, what you are here for and the legacy you want to leave behind.

These three chapters are entirely optional and you can skip them if you like, but they may help cement in that purpose statement a little more, so why not take a little journey through them?

PURPOSE STATEMENTS

Gael: *The purpose of my life is to love and give to inspire others.*

Courtney: *The purpose of my life is to be creative, courageous and passionate so I can write fiction to impact others by bringing them escape, entertainment and joy.*

Sasha: *The purpose of my life is to be authentic, compassionate and warm so that I can inspire, encourage and help people to be confidently and courageously themselves, actively living in the life they love.*

Karen: *The purpose of my life is to be passionate about what I do, be courageous when I feel fear, be authentic to myself, appreciate all that I have, relish the small joys, be generous with my knowledge, skills and time, be compassionate and kind to others and finally be mindful of my impact on the environment.*

8

DIVING DEEPER: TESTS

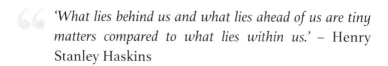'What lies behind us and what lies ahead of us are tiny matters compared to what lies within us.' – Henry Stanley Haskins

LET's GO DEEP

The next three chapters are:

- Tests – personality and values quizzes that reveal your characteristics
- Questions – queries that require thought-provoking answers about yourself
- Exercises – tasks that take a little more time to prompt insightful understanding of your inner workings

The tests are meant to be a bit of fun, to ease you into more of the navel-gazing work. The questions will challenge you to be truthful about the real you, and the exercises are designed to extract invaluable knowledge of your true self.

You can do these tests, questions and exercises split up over the course of a week or so or clear two hours and do them all at once.

I know I said 15 minutes, but what is a couple of hours in your long, long life?

You can skip the next three chapters, but here is why you may want to spend some of your valuable time reading them and then doing the tasks:

- You will get a deeper understanding of yourself in an overall sense.
- It will give you patterns and insights into your highest passions, values and strengths, which can help with day-to-day decisions and goal setting.
- With the above insights, you may revisit your purpose statement and tweak it to make it even more meaningful to you.
- The additional information gathered may help you supercharge your purpose with the tools detailed in Chapter Eleven.

The more you know about who you truly are, what motivates you, what you love to do and are great at, the clearer it will be to live a life of fulfillment and success.

GET IN STATE

First, please get into the right physical and mental state for this. Before doing any of these tasks:

- take three deep belly breaths
- scrunch your shoulders up to your ears tight and then release
- shake your whole body out
- put a smile on your face

Now pretend you are meeting YOU for the first time. You are open and ready to find out things. You are relaxed but also up for a challenge.

Make sure you have something to write, tap or type your answers on.

You are good to go.

Test Pros and Cons

There are many tests that look at people's personalities, characteristics and drivers. Each of them will give you some insight into yourself, but they also come with limitations. People worry the test will put them 'in a box' and define them according to archetypes that don't reflect the complex human they are. Conversely, people sometimes find that their results change over time or in a different mood or setting. Overall, there is a question of how valid the test results can be.

Still, sometimes tests tell you things about yourself or give you an insight or show you a pattern that you had never put together before.

Aren't you just a little curious what the tests will highlight?

Think of the results of the test as one tool in your toolbox, and combine it with the answers to the questions and the exercises to form a complete view of your essential self.

· · ·

Test Housekeeping

With all tests, it is suggested to carefully read your individual result and notice words and phrases that come up repeatedly. Then check if these relate to your purpose. Can your purpose be tweaked to incorporate these frequently used expressions that describe you?

You may find it is difficult to choose an answer to the test, so go with your gut or initial response.

Note that the websites may change or not be there at all. Some of the tests are free; some are no cost but require name and email details, and some of them require a payment. Whether a fee is charged and how much it is may be updated after this book is published as well.

All the following tests took between five and twenty minutes to do.

Myers-Briggs Type Indicator (MBTI) Personality Test

What is it?

From mbtionline.com: "Myers-Briggs...is designed to help you identify your preferred way of doing things in four key areas: directing and receiving energy, taking in information, making decisions, and approaching the outside world. Your natural preferences in these four areas sort into one of 16 distinct patterns of behavior called personality types."

What do the results look like?

You will end up with one of the 16 four-letter results that show your personality type, e.g.: ISTP or ENFJ.

WHY DO IT?

From mbtionline.com: "The assessment gives you a framework for understanding yourself and appreciating differences in others."

WHAT HAS IT GOT TO DO WITH FINDING MY PURPOSE?

This gives an overall—and scarily accurate—picture of you and your preferences. It will help you determine whether your purpose statement fits with your personality type.

WHERE TO DO THE TEST

At mbtionline.com the test is currently US$50.

At 16personalities.com the test is free as of the writing of this book.

KOLBE A INDEX

WHAT IS IT?

From kolbe.com: "[An] assessment identifying the natural way that people take action. Left to our own choice, each of us has an instinctive way of problem solving. Research shows that people are most productive when they are free to choose their own method of accomplishing a task or providing a solution."

. . .

WHAT DO THE RESULTS LOOK LIKE?

You will show preference in one or two of the four 'action modes': fact finder, follow through, quick start and implementer.

WHY DO IT?

From kolbe.com: "People who've taken the Kolbe Indexes have become more confident, more energetic, and more powerful - just from understanding their natural talents. Kolbe focuses on what's right with you and tells you how to build on it. Kolbe doesn't just help you achieve your goals; it helps you control your destiny."

WHAT HAS IT GOT TO DO WITH FINDING MY PURPOSE?

This test shows you your natural strengths used in creative problem solving. It will tap into how you can be the best version of you, exactly what your purpose is aiming for.

WHERE TO DO THE TEST

At kolbe.com the test is currently US$50.

Unfortunately there is no free version that is similar, but I highly recommend investing in this test.

THE FOUR TENDENCIES QUIZ

WHAT IS IT?

This short quiz, developed by author Gretchen Rubin, gives insight into how we respond to inner and outer expectations. It effectively answers how to get people—including ourselves—to do what we want.

What do the results look like?

Most people show strong preference in one of four tendencies: upholder, questioner, obliger or rebel.

Why do it?

From quiz.gretchenrubin.com: "Knowing our Tendency can help us set up situations in the ways that make it more likely that we'll achieve our aims. We can make better decisions, meet deadlines, meet our promises to ourselves, suffer less stress, and engage more deeply with others."

What has it got to do with finding my purpose?

It can help to decide how you would be best suited to impact others. For example, an upholder could inspire others with their methods to commit to expectations. A questioner could use their questioning skills to evoke change in an area that they feel strongly about.

Where to do the test

At quiz.gretchenrubin.com the test is free as of the writing of this book.

. . .

The 5 Love Languages Profile

What is it?

Author and marriage counselor, Gary Chapman, states that there are five love languages—different ways we prefer to give and receive love.

What do the results look like?

You will determine one or two primary love languages from the five types: words of affirmation, acts of service, receiving gifts, quality time and physical touch.

Why do it?

Discovering your primary love language will improve your connection to others.

What has it got to do with finding my purpose?

This test will help with your contribution part of purpose as it can show the best way you like to give. For instance, if you like words, then maybe you share your gifts through writing. If you prefer physical touch, you may decide to learn massage. If acts of service are most important, you may find yourself building schools in developing countries.

Where to do the test

At 5lovelanguages.com the test is free as of the writing of this book.

Tests about Strengths, Passions and Values

What are they?

The Fab List comes from an in-depth look at all the best strengths, passions and values that relate to the meaning of life. The tests below pull out these words and phrases in an order that relates to you personally.

Why do them?

During the 15-minute purpose exercise, you simply chose from The Fab List and The Impact Lists the words and phrases that are most important to you. The tests below will confirm whether the words that resonated with you during the 15-minute exercise are your highest-ranking strengths, passions and values.

There are many benefits. Even if you don't achieve your purpose, your life will be better for knowing and pursuing your passions. Positive psychology research confirms that using your strengths to work towards something creates a more meaningful and happy life. Knowing your values enables you to make space for what is most important to you in a guilt-free way.

What have they got to do with finding my purpose?

These tests will show you patterns of words and phrases that can be woven into your purpose if they are not there already. If the same words keep arising and they are not already in your purpose statement, you may want to revisit it and see if they belong there.

Where to do the tests

There are a number of different websites that offer these tests. Search 'strengths tests', 'passions tests' or 'values tests' and find one or two from the selection that suit your schedule and budget. These are three of the ones I took that were free at the time of writing this book:

- Strengths: VIA Strengths Finder - viacharacter.org (highly recommended)
- Passions: GeniusU - passiontest.geniusu.com
- Values: Barrett Value Centre - valuescentre.com

Phew!

I hope you have done at least some of the above tests. They are a useful tool to know yourself a little better, help refine your purpose and, of course, they can be a bit of fun as well.

If this has energized you, then flip to the next chapter and answer some of the deep questions about 'life, the universe and everything'.

If you wish to the look at my test results, check Appendix Two.

Purpose Statements

Shona: *The purpose of my life is to be fun and impact positively on others.*

Corey: *The purpose of my life is to connect and inspire people to be the best versions of themselves.*

Jennifer: *The purpose of my life is to be my authentic self, to live with love and joy in my heart and to serve.*

Rebecca: *The purpose of my life is to be authentic, kind and grow my own edges in order to empower others to be real and have a roll-on effect of creating greater understanding and unity in the world.*

9
———

DIVING DEEPER: QUESTIONS

 'Efforts and courage are not enough without purpose and direction.' – John F. Kennedy

Q&A

Below are questions that give you a good insight into YOU. By answering them you will see patterns of words plus phrases and notions that keep repeating. All the questions focus on your passions, strengths, and values plus what kind of impact or legacy you want to make.

The first step is to answer the questions, and the second step is to notice and highlight the main themes that emerge.

Put aside up to an hour, have no distractions and an open mind. You can tap your answers into your phone or type on a computer, but most people find an old-fashioned pen and paper works best for this. Handwriting seems to bypass a critical part of your brain. Some people write long-form paragraphs. Others prefer bullet points. Mind maps are often used. Do what feels right to you. The method you use to jot down the answers is not as important as the answers are.

You do not have to answer every question, but if you are resistant to answering a particular question, it can mean there is something important to dig out. There are a handful of questions per topic and some of them are similar but the different way they are written may just prompt an insightful answer. Write down whatever comes up without judgment. Remember, you don't have to show this to anyone.

Once the timer for writing finishes or you feel a natural conclusion, read over your answers and highlight common words and ideas. Check these against your purpose. Does your purpose statement reflect these in its own short way? If so, great. If not, look at tweaking it a little.

These questions are useful not just for refining your purpose but also for tapping into yourself, writing out your goals and so directing your future through your daily activities—what to say yes and no to. This will be discussed more in Chapter Eleven.

For now, let's get started!

Remember to take some deep breaths, release tension in your body and smile. Now you are in a great state to begin this challenging but ultimately satisfying undertaking.

CHILDHOOD QUESTIONS

- What did you love doing as a child?
- What did you want to be when you grew up? Why?
- What were you good at doing as a child and teenager?

- What are your most treasured memories from childhood?
- Think back to when you were younger: what just lit you up?
- What were your dreams when you were a child (say at 10 years old)?
- Have any passions stayed with you from childhood to adulthood? What ones?

Past Questions

- What parts of your life are you most satisfied with?
- What are the greatest moments of achievement or fulfillment in your life?
- What are some challenges, difficulties and hardships you have overcome?
- Excluding the major events of your life, what are three of your best memories?

Flow Questions

- What activities make you lose track of time?
- What were you doing last time you lost yourself in an activity?
- Remember when things felt on a roll or effortless: what were you doing?
- When was the last time you experienced a sense of timelessness and flow?

No Pay Questions

- What doesn't feel like work?
- What would you do even if nobody paid you?
- What would you do for a year if money were not an object?
- What would you spend time doing if you had complete financial abundance to do anything (after the mandatory 'hammock on the beach' period, of course)?

Fearless Questions

- If you were afraid of nothing, what would you do?
- What have you not tried because of your fear of failure or fear of success?
- Is there something that terrifies you but has always secretly captivated you?

Like or Love Questions

- What types of books do you read?
- What documentaries or films do you watch?
- What are you curious about or interested in?
- What do you love to do but hardly ever make time for?
- What subject could you read 10 books about without getting bored?

Energized Questions

- What drives you? Why?
- What tasks make you feel most energized?
- When was the last time you felt true excitement? Why?
- What gets you up in the morning and makes you feel most alive?
- What are the places, people and events that make you feel energized?

Joy Questions

- What are your most prized possessions? Why?
- What is something that can bring you to tears of joy?
- What activities do you absolutely love in your personal life?
- What makes you smile (people, events, hobbies, projects, etc.)?

Role Model Questions

- Who do you look up to and why?
- What characteristics do you most admire in people?
- Who is living the life you want, and who can you model/emulate?
- Who inspires you the most and why (friends, authors, artists, leaders, etc.)?

Strengths Questions

- What do you feel qualified to teach others?
- What do people always seem to ask you to help them with?
- What are you naturally good at (skills, abilities, talents, etc.)?
- What things do you do easily that seem to be difficult for other people?

Uniqueness Questions

- What things do you feel you are greatest at?
- What is the unique ability or gift you bring to the world?
- What do you do differently from everyone else that makes you stand out?
- What tools, technologies or online applications do you know how to use better than anyone else?

Work Questions

- What are the greatest sources of joy in your work?
- In what areas of work do you seem to get the best results?
- Where at work do you feel most confident and socially adept?

Future Questions

- What would you still like to achieve in life?

- What would you like your future memories to be?
- What would you regret not fully doing, being or having in your life?
- What do you currently not have in your life that you would appreciate having?

PROBLEM QUESTIONS

- What would you struggle for?
- What do you care about or what bothers you?
- What problems in the world do you want to fix?

IMPORTANCE QUESTIONS

- What matters most to you? Why?
- What is most important that you take for granted?
- What positive, uplifting, inspiring quotes do you refer to?
- What things do you care most deeply about and that transcend your immediate desires?

DESTINY QUESTIONS

- What do you want your life to be about?
- What kind of person do you ultimately want to become?
- What goals need to be accomplished to get the kind of life you want?
- If you could get one single message to your children,

your friends and family or a large group of people, what would it be?

Double Phew!

What a ride! These questions often bring up a whole heap of emotions. There may be tears. This is a good thing. You are tapping into the real you, and that is the only way you can really lean into your destiny.

Is your purpose statement feeling even more alive and relevant now? Good. That may give you the push you need to complete the exercises in the next chapter.

Purpose Statements

Melody: *The purpose of my life is to share love with others.*

Rita: *The purpose of my life is to be curious, joyful and healthy so that I can connect with and nurture others to contribute positively to my community.*

Diana: *The purpose of my life is to be healthy and full of life and to create abundance so that I can help others and can give my children all the tools they need to create their own happy and fulfilling lives.*

Valerie: *The purpose of my life is to live a wholesome life of my dreams, filled with magic of gratefulness and creation so that I can be the best of myself, charged and healthy and brave, open to wealth, freedom, wisdom, power and clarity, to be able to illuminate and make a difference around me and in the world.*

10

DIVING DEEPER: EXERCISES

 'The one thing you have that nobody else has is you. Your voice, your mind, your story, your vision. So write and draw and build and play and dance and live as only you can.' – Neil Gaiman

THE RICHES

You thought the questions were the hard part? Nup, sorry. They just scratched the surface. These exercises are challenging but boy do they dive down deep and bring up the greatest of treasures.

Take some deep breaths, shake your body out and try them if you dare...

1. YOUR IDEAL LIFE EXERCISE

Imagine you are living your ideal life, five, ten or twenty years from now. Give yourself 20 minutes and write out a description (writing by hand is recommended) of your perfect day where you are not on vacation, just a 'normal' day in your ideal life. To prompt you, answer these questions:

- What are you doing?
- What is a typical day like?
- What kind of work do you do?
- What have you accomplished?
- What things are you most proud of?
- Who and what do you have in your life?
- What do your home, family, work and relationships look like?

This exercise will tap into what you love, what is important to you and what kind of legacy you want to leave behind.

Look for themes and patterns in what you have written and check back in with your purpose statement. Does your purpose light the way to your ideal life?

2. What What What Exercise

For some people, even with the quick purpose exercise, the tests and the questions, a true purpose may remain elusive or not feel exactly right. This exercise is designed to extract it out, kicking and screaming if need be!

To get to your big WHY it has been argued that you shouldn't ask more 'why' questions but instead ask a series of WHAT questions.

Start with something, it could be big or small, that is important to you. Then ask:

What about X is important to me?

For example:

- What about keeping fit is important to me?
- What about being a great parent is important to me?
- What about having a successful business is important to me?

Then write out the first thing that comes into your head as a response to that question. I did this exercise for the 'keeping fit' question:

1. What about keeping fit is important to me?

   Answer: Keeping fit is important to me as I have more energy when I am fitter.

Then use the answer you have written down and ask the first question again: What about X is important to me? For example:

2. What about having more energy is important to me?

   Answer: Having more energy is important to me as I am able to do the work I want and be there for my family.

Here's the kicker—you need to keep asking this WHAT question at least FIVE to SEVEN times!

The first few answers will come from your head, but the next few will challenge you to be radically honest and come from your heart. This will almost always uncover something personal, genuine and fundamental about what drives you.

Even if you start with something small, by the time you are at least five layers deep you will find a very deep WHY for what you want to do. You will naturally arrive at your destination—your ultimate purpose.

Let's continue with my 'What What What' example for keeping fit:

3. What about doing the work I want and being there for my family is important to me?

Answer: I can feel successful in my work and home life.

4. What about feeling successful in my work and home life is important to me?

Answer: If I am successful I can inspire others to live their lives well.

5. What about inspiring others is important to me?

Answer: I can contribute to making the world a better place.

6. What about making the world a better place is important to me?

Answer: I will live well knowing that I have done my best.

Once you feel you have reached a natural end to the 'What What What' questions, check your five-to-seven-layer-deep 'what' answer to your purpose statement derived from the 15-minute exercise.

Do they marry up? Sometimes how much they correspond is uncanny.

Or do you need to refine your purpose slightly to incorporate this new understanding of yourself?

This is my purpose statement:

> 'The purpose of my life is to be my best self, full of love, energy and fun ('sparkle'), so I can continue to learn and create and then inspire others to achieve their potential'.

Obviously doing my best or being my best self is extremely important to me. Mmmm, interesting.

3. Write Your Own Obituary Exercise

The obituary exercise asks you to fast forward to the end of your life and then imagine that you are looking back over your time here on Earth. This works as a prompt as it stimulates urgency that the end of your life may be nearer than you think. This sounds a little morbid, but it will help pinpoint any areas for change and perhaps jolt you into action.

You do not have to follow the traditional format for an obituary. Think of it more as a prompt to define your ideal life and legacy. This exercise could also be called 'Write Your Own Eulogy', 'Write Your 100th Birthday Speech' or 'Write a Letter to Your Grandkids from Your Rocking Chair'. Don't get caught up in the semantics of what this exercise is called. Choose whichever works for you.

> It is the imagining of your big picture life that is the important part here.

Paint a picture of the person you want to be, of a life well lived. Look back at your life and all that you've achieved and acquired, all the relationships you have developed and what matters the most to you. Be specific and detailed but also grandiose.

Review different areas of your life such as health, family, work and contribution. Use words that inspire you. Start with what you have already accomplished and are proud of, and then move into your ambitions for the ideal future you.

Answer questions such as:

- Who have you impacted?
- What legacy are you leaving?
- What are you known or remembered for?
- What characteristics and qualities do you have?
- What are your quirks and charming idiosyncrasies?
- What specific things did you achieve in your lifetime?

If you are finding it hard to write all your positive attributes, greatest accomplishments and what you would be fondly remembered for, then ask yourself how you would NOT want to be thought of. What goals would you regret not having achieved?

What would you NOT want on your headstone?

I found the best way to do this was to write non-stop for at least three to ten minutes, answering the questions above and then adding anything else I thought of. Afterwards, I rewrote it all so it sounded like an obituary, organizing it so it highlighted what I enjoyed and achieved in the different areas of my life. See what I wrote as my obituary in Appendix Three.

Not only is this a valuable exercise to revisit your purpose statement, it is also an opportunity to get back on track, refocus your priorities and resurrect dreams that have become lost in the daily grind.

. . .

Triple Phew!

Didn't you have a blast getting to know yourself better?

What were the guts of it all? Do the patterns and themes that emerge from the tests, questions and exercises reflect your original purpose statement?

The odd person does a massive rewrite of their purpose, but most people say that they are happy with their 15-minute purpose statement, perhaps with a few minor tweaks here and there.

The final two chapters show you how you can supercharge your purpose plus explain why finding your purpose benefits us all.

Purpose Statements

> PJ: *The purpose of my life is to learn, discover and gain wisdom to empower my loved ones and serve others.*

> Haidee: *The purpose of my life is to be authentic and real, and to care and be there for others when they need it.*

> Jenny: *The purpose of my life is to enjoy creating mindfully, so I can write encouraging connection amongst older women.*

> Nandani: *The purpose of my life is to be playful, loving, be passionate, be grateful, to grow so that I can help, serve, empower and make a difference to the world I live in.*

11

SUPERCHARGE YOUR PURPOSE

 'I realized there are two things you take with you when you die. The love you've shared and the difference you've made.' – Jane Seymour

WHAT ELSE IS THERE?

You have your purpose statement, you believe it and are starting to live it. You may even have tackled the last three chapters and learned about yourself, your character and your motivations more deeply. Perhaps you used the additional information to tweak or add to your original 15-minute purpose statement.

What else can you possibly use your purpose statement and the greater understanding of inner workings for?

This chapter gives you two main options to supercharge your purpose. These are extras and there is no requirement to take them on, but if you are feeling energized with all this reflection work, you may want to attempt these two supercharging activities.

Purpose and Growth

An earlier chapter touched on the Six Human Needs and noted that the two secondary needs for growth and contribution are often not met as the four primary needs for certainty, variety, significance and love take precedence, especially your need for certainty.

One of the secondary needs is for growth. Although growth is evident everywhere from trees to babies, in this area it refers to using your strengths and abilities to work towards something, create something or improve yourself.

Growth is a natural force in the world and although many people resist it, we need it. As Victor Frankl states in *Man's Search for Meaning*: "What a man needs is not a tensionless state but rather the striving and struggling for a worthwhile goal, a freely chosen task."

Finding your purpose can be the catalyst to your much-needed growth. One way a purpose assists personal growth is to give you a tangible concept to refer to when you embark on goal setting.

For exactly why and how to set goals, I recommend reading my book, *Super Sexy Goal Setting*. Here is a quick summary to get you started: decide on four goals for the next 12 months. These should be exciting and meaningful to you (i.e.: 'sexy'). If you like, make a goal about each of the following: health, relationships, work/business and fun/just for you.

When you write out your goals make sure they align with your purpose statement. Now you have four super sexy goals that are aligned with your need for growth and with your purpose.

If that is not supercharged, I don't know what is.

Purpose and Contribution

You attain a meaningful life from a connection to a wider cause. In other words, by fulfilling the last of your six human needs, your need for contribution. The impact part of your purpose statement may be as simple as 'sharing my gifts with the world' or 'inspiring others'.

In order to supercharge your purpose for the contribution part, here is a simple way to make it crystal clear exactly WHO you want to serve and HOW you will help them. Note that you may or may not be paid for this service to the world.

Answer these three questions:

1. What do you like to do in which you have at least some expertise? Some call this their '10,000 hours skill', but I don't think you have to reach that level of mastery.
2. What does the community, tribe or audience that you want to impact need and want? In other words, what pain do they need healed? Or what joy would benefit them the most?
3. How are those people helped, or how do they transform or improve as a result of your contribution?

My answers:

1. Write books
2. Busy people who want more from life
3. Gain tools and wisdom to reach their potential

Then put it all together using a 'two-minute elevator pitch' role definition template that clearly states what you do and who benefits:

> I (your expertise) that help (description of people you help) so that they (transformation)

My two-minute elevator pitch:

> I write books that help busy people who want more from life so that they gain tools and wisdom to reach their potential.

The answers to these questions can and will change over time, so look at updating your two-minute elevator pitch each year when you review your purpose statement and write out your annual goals.

Purpose Statements

> Natalie: *The purpose of my life is to be happy, to enjoy and appreciate every moment, so that I can empower and love others unconditionally.*

> Edyta: *The purpose of my life is to be healthy, happy and have freedom so that I can grow, create and achieve, and then inspire other people to success.*

> Sue: *The purpose of my life is to be positive, live with meaning and purpose, give support and help to others by inspiring wellbeing, enjoy the loved ones who provide so much joy.*

Rach: *The purpose of my life is to achieve massive success, with sheer determination, whilst maintaining peace and honoring my soul, I in turn share my gifts with others to empower, inspire and assist them to fulfill their dreams.*

12

WHAT IS THE PURPOSE OF A BOOK ON PURPOSE?

 'Happiness is like a butterfly, the more you chase it, the more it will evade you, but if you notice the other things around you, it will gently come and sit on your shoulder.' – Henry David Thoreau

KNOW THYSELF

The purpose of this book about finding your purpose (very meta!) is simple: to help you to know yourself better.

Sure, a 15-minute exercise to find your purpose may not be the deepest navel-gazing you will ever do, but it is a start. You may never look at your purpose again, but if you have discovered one more thing about yourself that helps you live better, then this book has met its purpose.

Of course, I would love everyone to not only find a purpose, believe it and start living it, but also do the other tasks—the tests, questions and exercises. These allow you to take some time checking in and getting to know yourself better. I truly believe that understanding the core of you will help in your life, relationships and work.

As author and businesswoman, Arianna Huffington states in *Thrive*: "We are not on this earth to accumulate victories or trophies but to be whittled down until what is left is who we truly are."

BENEFITS OF HAVING A PURPOSE FOR YOU

You may have already noticed some of the benefits of having a purpose such as:

- You feel more certain in yourself as you become more focused on what you want to be and clear about what you really want to do.
- You have a sense of direction, a path, an exciting journey to a meaningful destination.
- A purpose gets you out of bed with resilience and energy that come from within.
- Having a purpose means living for today, not for some end game, or even worse, someone else's game.
- A purpose allows you to be more compassionate to both yourself and others.
- Purpose is a primary key to strong mental health as you know you are here for a reason.
- Your purpose leads to healing and fulfillment as you feel like your life is about something bigger than just yourself.

As Jen Sincero says in *You are a Badass*: "It is about getting clear on what makes you happy and what makes you feel most alive and then creating that instead of pretending you can't have it or don't deserve it."

BENEFITS OF HAVING A PURPOSE FOR THE WORLD

Having a purpose with a contribution element has an immeasurable effect on the world. There is only one unique YOU. You are the only YOU there ever will be. It makes no sense to hide, to play small and to not be generous.

> There is absolutely no doubt the world is improved by you sharing your gifts.

Don't deny the world your magnificence. We are not here to fit in but to be different and add a small piece of ourselves to the mosaic of life. Add service to your life. People want to be part of something that makes a difference.

I envisage that if everyone operates from their truest passions, strengths and values, the world will be a better place.

Media company CEO, Tim O'Reilly couldn't have said it any better: "Pursue something so important that even if you fail, the world is better off with you having tried."

THE TRUTH

The truth is that it doesn't actually matter whether you know for sure if you are living your real purpose in life.

The truth is that living deliberately leads in a roundabout way to true happiness.

The truth is that life is NOT short. Life is the longest thing we have. It is disrespectful to not at least try and make it the masterpiece we wish it to be.

When you decide to show up, take action and do some good in the world it is almost impossible for love, joy and success not to accompany you on your purpose-driven journey.

Dream big. Laugh often. Take a deep breath and just have a go.

Your Purpose Statement

Here is my purpose again:

> *The purpose of my life is to be my best self, full of love, energy and fun ('sparkle'), so I can continue to learn and create and then inspire others to achieve their potential.*

What is your purpose? I would love to hear it. If you want to share it with me, shoot me a quick email: julie@julieschooler.com.

The purpose of my life is to _____

APPENDIX ONE – FIND YOUR PURPOSE IN 15 MINUTES SUMMARY

Purpose Recap

Your purpose is your WHY for being here. It is what you live for, what is important to you and what makes your life significant and worthwhile.

A purpose statement should be short, positive and powerfully resonate with you. The template below is a useful foundation that can also be rearranged to fit your unique purpose statement.

> **Definition:** Your purpose is about who you want to BE and what you want to DO so that you have an IMPACT on others.

> **Template:** 'The purpose of my life is to (be and/or do) _____ to (impact) _____.'

E.g.: The purpose of my life is to be courageous, abundance-oriented and full of gratitude so that I can share my gifts with others and help the environment.

E.g.: The purpose of my life is to be full of passion so I can use my determination and inquisitive nature to help to make a difference in my community and the world.

The Words Lists

One of the most difficult parts of finding your purpose is coming up with the right words to use. The 15-minute purpose exercise makes things super easy for you by giving you all the words you need for the BE, DO and IMPACT elements.

Use any of the words. They are displayed in a manner that is meant to make them easier to read and choose, not because the 'main' word is more important than the associated words and phrases.

Feel free to highlight all the words you like. Then try and narrow down to the most important ones for you. It is okay to drop a few of the words when writing out your purpose statement. They won't mind.

You may need to change the words slightly to fit into your purpose statement ('love' to 'loving', 'create' to 'creative', 'power' to 'powerful', etc.).

If you have a word not in the lists that best suits your purpose, please use it. People say these lists nudge them to come up with other words, or they add a faith-based component as well.

Find Your Purpose in 15 Minutes Instructions

1. Take a deep breath and say in an excited voice: 'I will find my purpose today!'

2. Keep this purpose statement template in mind:

'The purpose of my life is to (be and/or do) _____ to (impact) _____'

3. Read **The Fab List** below and highlight or write down any words that resonate the most with you. Most people eventually settle on between 2 and 8 words:

- Love – nice, kind, caring, grace
- Healthy – energy, vitality, wellbeing, fit, strong
- Happy – joy, cheerful, positive, optimistic, fulfilled
- Fun – enjoy, playful, humor, laughter
- Grow – learn, discover, improve, master, knowledge
- Achieve – accomplish, success, excellence, live my dreams
- Create – imagine, innovate, invent, art
- Courage – brave, confident, bold, adventurous, face fear
- Passionate – excitement, enthusiastic, zest for life
- Give – help, contribute, serve, generous, benevolent
- Peace – calm, simplicity, tranquil, serene, rest
- Curious – inquisitive, interested, wonder, be in awe
- Spiritual – aware, conscious, wholeness, mindful, transcendent
- Integrity – fair, honest, sincere, true, open
- Authentic – real, genuine, be me, be myself, be true to me
- Ideal self – be my best self, reach my potential, be a good person
- Appreciate – gratitude, grateful, thankful, treasure
- Compassionate – supportive, considerate, empathetic, thoughtful, warm
- Persistent – determined, driven, motivated, ambitious, grit
- Abundance – wealth, freedom, beauty, wisdom, power

4. Read the **Impact Lists** below and highlight or write down the verbs and nouns that fit the impact part of your purpose statement. Most people choose between 1 and 3 words from each list:

Verbs

- Give – help, gift, provide, give abundance to
- Share – serve, share my gifts, contribute, nourish, delight
- Connect – teach, write, speak, learn, read
- Lead – empower, inspire, encourage, spread magic, focus on
- Accept – listen, understand, heal, forgive
- Make a difference – give hope to, work towards, stand for, challenge

Nouns

- Non-specific – others, humans, all beings, people, creatures
- Specific – organizations, causes, charities, community, groups
- Friends and Family – loved ones, my family, my children, my tribe
- General – the world, the environment, nature, my legacy

5. Take out a pen and paper and write out

   'The purpose of my life is to ____'

6. Add your favorite words from **The Fab List** and the **Impact Lists** into the template and rewrite your purpose statement until it powerfully resonates with you. This may take a handful of attempts but you WILL get there.

7. Read your final purpose statement aloud.

Congratulations, just like that you have found your purpose!

APPENDIX TWO – MY TEST RESULTS

I took the tests discussed in Chapter Eight, so if you are curious about my test results, here are the main ones:

Myers-Briggs Type Indicator (MBTI) Personality Test

Test taken via 16personalities.com – free during the writing of this book

Current test result: ENFJ

Previously identified with INFJ and ISFJ

Kolbe A Index

Test taken via kolbe.com – currently US$50

My Kolbe action style: High on 'Fact finder' and 'Follow through'

The Four Tendencies Quiz

Test taken via quiz.gretchenrubin.com - free during the writing of this book

Tendency: Upholder

The 5 Love Languages Profile

Test taken via 5lovelanguages.com - free during the writing of this book

Love language: Quality Time and Words of Affirmation

The VIA Strengths Finder

Test taken via viacharacter.org - free during the writing of this book

Top three highest strengths: love of learning, gratitude, industry, diligence and perseverance

Top three lowest strengths: bravery and valor, modesty and humility, forgiveness and mercy

APPENDIX THREE – MY OBITUARY EXERCISE

Julie lived to a ripe old age and accomplished a lot over her lifetime. She truly lived her life with purpose, motivated to be her best self, full of sparkle, and used her gifts to encourage others to do the same.

She valued and exuded the following qualities wherever she could: love, joy, contribution, beauty, inspiration, wisdom, energy, health, integrity, fun, creativity, success and abundance.

Health and fitness were important to Julie—she enjoyed challenging herself to be as strong and as full of energy as she could so she could keep up with her work commitments... and her grandkids!

Having meaningful relationships as a wife, mama, sister, daughter, friend or business colleague were of utmost value. Spending time with family and friends was a major part of Julie's life. She loved fun days at the beautiful locations near where she lived and the events, dinners and casual get-togethers that she often arranged.

Julie started writing and publishing books out of an innate drive to be creative after her first child was born. This developed into a successful business through which Julie was constantly learning and sharing wisdom about life, love and what is truly important via blogging, courses, speaking and coaching.

She loved seeing how creative she could be so also wrote children's picture books, novels and turned out other products that were imaginative, beautiful and fun.

Travel was a great love and Julie travelled extensively, visiting exotic places and relaxing in many tropical locations. Her kids still remember that fantastic Disneyland holiday when they were young, and her best friends fondly remember her 50th birthday celebrations across France—a lot of champagne was consumed on that trip!

Everyone knows how much Julie loved going after and achieving meaningful goals. She especially liked checking things off her long bucket list. The 40 things she checked off her 'Top40 Bucket List' the year she turned 40 were just the start.

Although she worked hard, Julie also made time for fun as she knew it was the key to a fulfilling life. She enjoyed indulging in doorstop novels, going to the cinema, dancing like an idiot and playing with her children and grandchildren. She sometimes showed her dark sense of humor and also loved being ridiculously silly on occasion.

Having an abundance mindset was a major focus of Julie's and she contributed to the world in a myriad of ways—giving to charity, helping out in the community and always having a listening ear plus a cup of tea or glass of wine ready for family, friends or other mamas when it was needed.

Julie always said she wanted to feel like that her life meant something. Her greatest wish was to leave her mark on the world so it would be a better place to live in simply due to the fact that she was here. I think we can all agree that her wish was granted.

READER GIFT: THE HAPPY20

There is no doubt that creating a bucket list, setting goals and finding your purpose will change your life, but it is also important to remember to squeeze the best out every single day. To remind you of this, I created

THE HAPPY20
20 Free Ways to Boost Happiness in 20 Seconds or Less

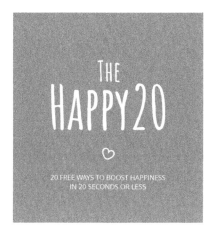

A PDF gift for you with quick ideas to improve mood and add a little sparkle to your day.

Head to **JulieSchooler.com/gift** and grab your copy today.

ABOUT THE AUTHOR

Julie had aspirations of being a writer since she was very young but somehow got sidetracked into the corporate world. After the birth of her first child, she rediscovered her creative side. You can find her at JulieSchooler.com.

Her *Easy Peasy* books provide simple and straightforward information on parenting topics. The *Nourish Your Soul* series shares delicious wisdom to feel calmer, happier and more fulfilled.

Busy people can avoid wasting time searching for often confusing and conflicting advice and instead spend time with the beautiful tiny humans in their lives and do what makes their hearts sing.

Julie lives with her family in a small, magnificent country at the bottom of the world where you may find her trying to bake the perfect chocolate brownie.

 facebook.com/JulieSchoolerAuthor
instagram.com/julie.schooler
 twitter.com/JulieSchooler

BOOKS BY JULIE SCHOOLER

Easy Peasy **Books**

Easy Peasy Potty Training

Easy Peasy Healthy Eating

Nourish Your Soul **Books**

Rediscover Your Sparkle

Crappy to Happy

Embrace Your Awesomeness

Bucket List Blueprint

Super Sexy Goal Setting

Find Your Purpose in 15 Minutes

Clutter-Free Forever

Children's Picture Books

Maxy-Moo Flies to the Moon

Collections

Change Your Life 3-in-1 Collection

Rebelliously Happy 3-in-1 Collection

JulieSchooler.com/books

ACKNOWLEDGMENTS

To Andrew and our two beautiful tiny humans, Dylan and Eloise.
I live in a perpetual state of astonishment about how fortunate
my life is. Thank you for making me laugh every single day.

PLEASE LEAVE A REVIEW

Change Your Life 3-in-1 Collection

Bucket List Blueprint, Super Sexy Goal Setting, Find Your Purpose in 15 Minutes

THANK YOU FOR READING THIS BOOK

I devoted many months to researching and writing this book. I then spent more time having it professionally edited, working with a designer to create an awesome cover and launching it into the world.

Time, money and heart has gone into this book and I very much hope you enjoyed reading it as much as I loved creating it.

It would mean the world to me if you could spend a few minutes writing a review on Goodreads or the online store where you purchased this book.

A review can be as short or long as you like and should be helpful and honest to assist other potential buyers of the book.

Reviews provide social proof that people like and recommend the book. More book reviews mean more book sales which means I can write more books.

Your book review helps me, as an independent author, more than you could ever know. I read every single review and when I get five-star review it absolutely makes my day.

Thanks, Julie.

BOOK REFERENCES

59 Seconds – Change Your Life in Under a Minute – Richard Wiseman (USA, 2011)

Achieving Your Best Self – Fast Track Your Efforts to Achieving Your Highest Goals – Dr. David Barton (NZ, 2016)

Authentic Happiness – Using the New Positive Psychology to Realize Your Potential for Lasting Fulfillment – Martin Seligman, Ph.D. (US, 2002)

Feel the Fear and Do It Anyway – How to Turn Your Fear and Indecision into Confidence and Action – Susan Jeffers (UK, 1987)

Finding Your Own North Star – How to Claim the Life You Were Meant to Live – Martha Beck (US, 2001)

Finding Your Way in a Wild New World – Reclaim Your True Nature to Create the Life You Want – Martha Beck (US, 2012)

Find Your Why – A Practical Guide for Discovering Purpose for You and Your Team – Simon Sinek, David Mead, Peter Docker (US, 2017)

Life on Purpose – How Living for What Matters Most Changes Everything – Victor J. Strecher (US, 2016)

Man's Search for Meaning – Victor E. Frankl (US, 1959 / 2006)

Minimalism – Live a Meaningful Life – Joshua Fields Millburn and Ryan Nicodemus (US, 2016)

Start With Why – How Great Leaders Inspire Everyone to Take Action – Simon Sinek (US, 2009)

Steering by Starlight – The Science and Magic of Finding Your Destiny – Martha Beck (US, 2008)

Succeed – How We Can Reach Our Goals with the Nine Things Successful People Do Differently – Heidi Grant Halvorson, Ph.D. (US, 2010)

The Four Disciplines of Execution – Achieving Your Wildly Important Goals – C McChesney, S Covey, J Huling (US, 2012)

The Destiny Formula – Find Your Purpose. Overcome Your Fear of Failure. Use Your Natural Talents and Strengths to Build a Successful Life – Ayodeji Awosika (US, 2015)

The Five Love Languages – The Secret to Love that Lasts – Gary Chapman (US, 1992 / 2010)

The Happiness of Pursuit – Finding the Quest that Will Bring Purpose to Your Life – Chris Guillebeau (US, 2014)

The Happiness Project – Gretchen Rubin (USA, 2009)

The Life You Were Born to Live – A Guide to Finding Your Life Purpose – Dan Millman (US, 1993)

The One Goal – Master the Art of Goal Setting, Win Your Inner Battles and Achieve Exceptional Results – Thibaut Meurisse (US, 2017)

The ONE Thing – The surprisingly simple truth behind extraordinary results – Gary Keller with Jay Papasan (US, 2013)

The Secret – Rhonda Byrne (US, 2006)

The Seven Habits of Highly Effective People – Restoring the Character Ethic – Steven R Covey (US, 1990)

*The Subtle Art of Not Giving a F*ck – A Counterintuitive Approach to Living a Good Life* – Mark Manson (US, 2016)

The Top Five Regrets of the Dying – A Life Transformed by the Dearly Departed – Bronnie Ware (US, 2011)

The Winner's Bible – Rewire Your Brain for Permanent Change – Dr Kerry Spackman (USA, 2009)

The Zigzag Principle – The Goal-Setting Strategy that will Revolutionize Your Business and Your Life – Rich Christiansen (US, 2012)

Thrive – The Third Metric to Redefining Success and Creating a Life of Wellbeing, Wisdom and Wonder – Arianna Huffington (US, 2014)

What Matters Most – Living a More Considered Life – James Hollis, PhD (US, 2009)

You are a Badass – How to Stop Doubting Your Greatness and Start Living an Awesome Life – Jen Sincero (US, 2013)

Printed in Great Britain
by Amazon